PRAISE FOR

# THE *Dressmaker* OF *Khair Khana*

Care corso

"Remarkable."

—*The New Yorker*

"A transporting, enlightening book. . . . *The Dressmaker of Khair Khana* is a fascinating window on Afghan life under the Taliban and a celebration of women the world over who support their loved ones with tenacity, inventiveness, and sheer guts."

—*People*

"*The Dressmaker of Khair Khana* is pure inspiration. . . . It reveals in acute detail the anxiety of ordinary people trying to fold their lives around the whims and laws of abusive regimes."

—*Los Angeles Times*

"*The Dressmaker of Khair Khana* gives voice to many of our world's unsung heroines. Against all odds, these young women created hope and community, and they never gave up. This book is guaranteed to move you—and to show you a side of Afghanistan few ever see."

—Angelina Jolie

"An Afghan family finds a way to survive in Kabul under Taliban rule in this awe-inspiring true story. Fans of *Three Cups of Tea* are sure to embrace this powerful and humbling book."

—*Parade*

"Gayle Tzemach Lemmon tells a true, inspiring story of courageous women and quiet heroism at work in Taliban-era Afghanistan."

—*Christian Science Monitor*

"Gayle Tzemach Lemmon embroiders the life of the 'Dressmaker of Khair Khana,' the remarkable story of an ingenious young Afghan woman who, under the Taliban's rule, created jobs for a hundred women."

—*Vanity Fair*

"A riveting and important book."    N- Tajik

—*Fast Company*

Inshallah                     S- Pashtun

"A courageous Afghan woman and her sisters succeed as unlikely entrepreneurs in this inspiring true story."                    —*O, The Oprah Magazine*

"Books on Afghanistan usually fall into one of two categories: policy-oriented polemics or simple tales about do-gooders. Rarely has an author been so successful in turning on-the-ground reportage into a dramatic and yet deeply informative story. *The Dressmaker of Khair Khana* reads like great fiction and yet it is all true; this book will grab you from the first sentence and take you on an amazing journey that crosses many borders: cultural, geographical, intellectual, and, most importantly, emotional. It is a must-read."      —Mohamed El-Erian, author of *When Markets Collide*

"A fascinating story that touches on family, gender, business, and politics and offers inspiration through the resourceful, determined woman at its heart."                                                                 —*Publishers Weekly*

"An inspiring story of courageous community-building. . . . [Lemmon] pays scrupulous attention to detail . . . [and] convincingly evokes the atmosphere of Taliban-era Kabul."                              —*Kirkus Reviews*

"Lemmon tells the riveting true story of Kamila Sidiqi and other women of Afghanistan in the wake of the Taliban's rise to power."
                                                                        —*Business Insider*

"Gayle Lemmon's riveting portrait of Kamila, told with grace, elegance, and passion, captures the extraordinary tenacity and ingenuity of one woman who quietly triumphed under the Taliban for the sake of her family. A powerful read that serves as a reminder that Afghanistan can never thrive until it embraces the active involvement of women—with their resourcefulness, spirit, and resilience—in its leadership and future."
                                                                        —Tina Brown

"[Kamila Sidiqi] picked up a needle and thread, a whole lot of courage, and became an entrepreneur with her own dressmaking business. She offered work to a hundred other local women, forging bonds among oppressed women and creating a real community in very trying times."
                                                                        —*New York Post*

"Nothing short of amazing. . . . Definitely a must-read!"  —MSN *Glo*

"A small and unassuming book about young women entrepreneurs who find ways to work around the cruel Taliban restrictions in Kabul will nonetheless read as revolutionary. By writing about women who take great risks and achieve relative success, [Lemmon] equips women around the world with something real they can use to improve their lives and make a difference for other women, as well."

—Gatehouse News Service

"By sharing these women's courageously tenacious stories, Lemmon provides readers convincing proof to believe, as well."  —*BookDragon*

"Lemmon's storytelling is her strength—the way the book is organized is captivating. Make no mistake that *The Dressmaker of Khair Khana* has solid journalistic chops and remains based in fact. It is a feel-good, pleasurable read at the crossroads between journalism and novel."

—*Muslimah Media Watch*

"The *Dressmaker of Khair Khana* is a most remarkable tale."

—*Pittsburgh Post-Gazette*

"Kamila's story is a truly inspiring one and a testament to the ingenuity and resiliency of the human spirit."  —*BurdaStyle*

"*The Dressmaker of Khair Khana* is a captivating wartime adventure story, but it is also a lesson in tenacity and courage."  —Acton Institute

# The Dressmaker of Khair Khana

HARPER PERENNIAL

NEW YORK • LONDON • TORONTO • SYDNEY • NEW DELHI • AUCKLAND

THE

# *Dressmaker*

OF

# *Khair Khana*

✳

FIVE SISTERS,

ONE REMARKABLE FAMILY,

AND THE WOMAN WHO RISKED

EVERYTHING TO KEEP THEM SAFE

## Gayle Tzemach Lemmon

HARPER PERENNIAL

A hardcover edition of this book was published in 2011 by HarperCollins Publishers.

P.S.™ is a trademark of HarperCollins Publishers.

THE DRESSMAKER OF KHAIR KHANA. Copyright © 2011 by Gayle Tzemach Lemmon.
All rights reserved. Printed in the United States of America. No part of this
book may be used or reproduced in any manner whatsoever without
written permission except in the case of brief quotations embodied
in critical articles and reviews. For information address
HarperCollins Publishers, 10 East 53rd Street, New York, NY 10022.

HarperCollins books may be purchased for educational, business, or sales
promotional use. For information please write: Special Markets Department,
HarperCollins Publishers, 10 East 53rd Street, New York, NY 10022.

FIRST HARPER PERENNIAL EDITION PUBLISHED 2012.

*Designed by Jennifer Daddio / Bookmark Design & Media Inc.*

*Map by Nick Springer, Springer Cartographics LLC*

The Library of Congress has catalogued the hardcover edition as follows:

Tzemach Lemmon, Gayle.
    The dressmaker of Khair Khana : five sisters, one remarkable family, and the
woman who risked everything to keep them safe / Gayle Tzemach Lemmon.—
1st ed.
    p.   cm.
    Includes bibliographical references.
    ISBN 978-0-06-173237-9 (hardcover)
    ISBN 978-0-06-207220-7 (international edition)
    1. Sidiqi, Kamila, 1977- 2. Sidiqi, Kamila, 1977—Family. 3. Khair
Khana (Kabul, Afghanistan)—Biography. 4. Kabul (Afghanistan)—
Biography. 5. Dressmakers—Afghanistan—Kabul—Biography. 6. Sisters—
Afghanistan—Kabul—Biography. 7. Businesswomen—Afghanistan—
Kabul—Biography. 8. Community life—Afghanistan—Kabul—History—21st
century. 9. Kabul (Afghanistan)—Social life and customs—21st century.
10. Kabul (Afghanistan)—Economic conditions—21st century. I. Title.
DS375.K2T94  2011
958.1—dc22
[B]
                                                          2010020774

ISBN 978-0-06-173247-8 (pbk.)

12 13 14 15 16 OV/RRD  10 9 8 7 6 5 4 3 2 1

To

ALL THOSE WOMEN

whose stories will never be told,

and to

RHODA TZEMACH

and

FRANCES SPIELMAN

# Author's Note

The stories in this book reflect three years of on-the-ground interviews and research in Kabul, London, and Washington, D.C. Security in Afghanistan has deteriorated during this time. I have changed the names of many of the characters in the pages that follow for the sake of their safety or out of respect for their desire for privacy. When requested, I have also omitted less relevant details that would make the book's characters readily identifiable. I have worked hard to ensure the accuracy of the dates and times attached to their histories, but I admit that their precision may be slippery given just how much Afghanistan has seen in the past three decades and the years that have passed since this story began.

# Contents

Introduction      xi

1   The News Arrives and Everything Changes      1

2   A Time of Good-byes      21

3   Stitching the Future Back Together      39

4   The Plan Goes to Market      64

5   An Idea Is Born . . . but Will It Work?      92

6   Class Is in Session      116

7   An Unexpected Wedding Party      141

8   A New Opportunity Knocks      165

9   Danger in the Night Sky      194

    Epilogue: Kabul Jan, Kaweyan, and Kamila's Faith in Good Fortune      217

Acknowledgments      235

Select Bibliography      243

Resources      253

# *Introduction*

I touched down in Afghanistan for the first time on a raw winter morning in 2005 after two days of travel that took me from Boston to Dubai via London. My eyes stung and my head whirled. Too anxious to sleep, I had stayed up all night in Dubai's Terminal II waiting for the Ariana flight to Kabul, scheduled to depart at 6:30 A.M. The Afghan airline urged travelers to arrive three hours early, which made finding a hotel feel somewhat beside the point. The predawn destinations on the big black travel board read like a guide to the world's exotic hot spots: Karachi, Baghdad, Kandahar, Luanda. I realized I was the only woman in the airport, and, perched on a corner window ledge in the sparsely furnished Terminal II lobby waiting for my cell phone to charge, I tried hard to make myself invisible. But I could feel the puzzled stares of the men dressed in their loose-fitting *shalwar kameez* as they passed me by, pushing their rented silver luggage trolleys

stacked high with bulging suitcases that were bound together with heavy brown cord. I imagined them wondering what in the world is that young woman doing here all
alone at three o'clock in the morning?

To be honest, I wondered, too. I snuck into the empty
but freshly cleaned ladies' room to change from my Boston
outfit of gray turtleneck, Kasil jeans, and English brown
leather boots, into an oversize pair of black pants, black
long-sleeved T-shirt, black Aerosoles, and black socks.
My only color concession was a loose-fitting rust-colored
sweater I had purchased at a New Age crystal shop in
Cambridge, Massachusetts. My friend Aliya had lent me
a black wool headscarf, and I struggled to casually toss it
over my head and shoulders, as she had taught me when
we were sitting together on a plush couch thousands of
miles—and worlds—away in her dorm room at Harvard
Business School. Now, twenty-five hours later, standing
alone in a sterile restroom in Dubai, I draped and re-
draped my shawl a dozen times until I got it passably right.
I looked in the mirror and didn't recognize myself. "Oh,
it's fine," I said out loud to my worried-looking reflection.
"The trip will be great." Faking confidence, I turned on
my rubber wedge heel and walked out of the ladies' room.

Eight hours later I descended the metal staircase onto
the makeshift tarmac at Kabul International Airport. The
sun shone brightly and the scent of charred winter air—
crisp, but laced with fumes—went straight to my nose. I

bumbled along, trying to keep Aliya's wool scarf in place as I dragged my orange carry-on behind me. I had to stop every few feet to adjust my veil. No one had prepared me for how hard it was to stay covered while in motion, let alone when lugging heavy baggage. How did the women all around me manage it so gracefully? I wanted to be like them, but instead I looked ridiculous, a goofy foreign duckling fumbling among the local swans.

I waited for an hour in the 1960s-style airport, mesmerized by the carcasses of Russian tanks that still sat along the side of the runway, decades after the Soviets had left Afghanistan. I managed to get through the passport line quickly and without incident. So far, so good, I thought. But then, having gotten through customs, everyone around me quickly began to disperse in different directions, displaying a sense of purpose that I distinctly lacked. I felt a sharp stab of anxiety shoot through my stomach as I realized that I had no idea what to do or where to go. Journalists who travel to faraway and dangerous places usually work with "fixers," local men and women who arrange their travel, interviews, and lodgings. Mine, a young man named Mohamad, was nowhere to be found. I fumbled through my wallet for his phone number, helpless and frightened but trying to look cool and collected. Where could he be? I wondered. Had he forgotten the American, the former ABC News producer, he had promised by email to pick up at the airport?

At last I found his mobile number on a piece of crumpled paper at the bottom of my purse. But I had no way to call him; I had dutifully charged my UK cell phone, but my London SIM card didn't work here in Kabul. So much for preparation.

Ten minutes went by, then twenty. Still no Mohamad. I imagined myself, five days later, still stuck at the Kabul Airport. As Afghan families cheerfully hurried out the glass doors, I felt more lonely than I had at 3 A.M. in Dubai's Terminal II. Only the unsmiling British soldiers milling around massive NATO tanks in front of the airport brought me any comfort. Worst-case scenario, I thought: I could go to the Brits and ask them to take me in. Never before had I found the sight of a tank at an airport reassuring.

Finally, I spotted a twentysomething bearded man selling phone cards, candies, and juices at a little corner stand by the airport's front door. I broke out a five-dollar bill and a big smile and asked in English if I could use his phone. He smiled and handed it over.

"Mohamad," I cried, shouting loudly to be certain he could hear me. "Hello, hello, this is Gayle, the American journalist. I am at the airport. Where are you?"

"Hello, Gayle," he said, calmly. "I'm in the parking lot; I've been here the past two hours. We can't come any closer because of security. Just follow the crowds; I'll be waiting for you."

Of course, security restrictions. How could I not have thought of that?

I pushed my own overstuffed silver luggage cart the length of two football fields to a parking lot miles away from the NATO tanks and their British soldiers. There, as promised, was Mohamad, smiling warmly.

"Welcome to Kabul," he said, grabbing my green Eddie Bauer duffel crammed full of headlamps, long johns, and wool blankets I had bought just for this trip. I wondered how many naïve foreigners Mohamad had greeted at the airport like this. He had worked with journalists for years and was a journalist in his own right. A friend at CBS News in London had insisted I hire him because she knew he was professional, experienced, and trustworthy—exactly what I would need in Kabul in the winter of 2005, a time when occasional rocket attacks and bombings had begun escalating into a full-blown insurgency. At that moment I felt most grateful for her insistence.

The streets of the Afghan capital were a cacophonous free-for-all, with crutch-bearing amputees, taped-together cars, donkeys, fuel-towing bicycles, and United Nations SUVs all fighting for the right-of-way with no traffic lights to guide them and only a smattering of police governing their progress. The crunchy grime of the brown Kabul air clung to everything—lungs, sweaters, headscarves, and windows. It was a noxious souvenir of decades of war in which everything, from the trees to the sewage system, had been destroyed.

I had never seen such an urban Wild West. Drivers would nudge the front end of their vehicles to within two inches of our blue Toyota Corolla, then suddenly careen back into their own lane. Afghan music blared from the Toyotas, Hondas, and Mercedes that were stuck with us in the gridlock. The city was clamorous in honking horns. White-haired old men with woolen blankets draped loosely across their shoulders stepped in front of cars, halting traffic and paying no attention to the oncoming vehicles. Clearly they—and everyone else—were used to this mad jumble of barely managed chaos that was Kabul.

I was not. I was a first-timer.

I was on winter break during my second year of MBA study at Harvard Business School. Journalism had always been my first love, but a year earlier I had given up my job covering presidential campaigns for the ABC News Political Unit, where I had spent much of my adult life. At thirty, I took the leap and decided to pursue my passion for international development, certain that if I didn't leave then, I never would. So I shed the warm cocoon of my Washington, D.C., world for graduate school. The first thing I did was start hunting for a subject rich with stories that no one else was covering. Stories that mattered to the world.

The issue that called me was women who work in

war zones: a particularly intrepid and inspiring form of entrepreneurship that happens regularly right in the heart of the world's most dangerous conflicts—and their aftermath.

I began my research in Rwanda. I went there to see firsthand how women play a part in rebuilding their country by creating business opportunities for themselves and others. Women accounted for three-quarters of Rwanda's citizens immediately after the 1994 genocide; a decade later, they remained the majority. International officials— all men—in the capital city of Kigali told me there was no story: that women did not own small businesses in Rwanda, that they worked only in the far less lucrative microfinance sector selling fruit and handicrafts at little stands on the side of the road. My reporting showed me they were wrong: I found women who owned gas stations and ran hotels. And the fruit sellers I interviewed were exporting their avocados and bananas to Europe twice a week. Shortly afterward I published a profile in the *Financial Times* of some of the most successful entrepreneurs I'd met—including a businesswoman selling baskets to Macy's, the famous New York department store chain.

Now, just a few months later, I was in Kabul, again for the *Financial Times*, to report on a surprising phenomenon: a new generation of Afghan businesswomen who had emerged in the wake of the Taliban's takeover. I had also promised to find a protagonist for a case study that

Harvard Business School would teach the following year. My former network news colleagues had tried to help me prepare for Kabul and paved the way by sharing their contacts, but as soon as I arrived I realized just how little I actually knew about the country.

All I had was the passionate desire to pursue a story.

Most stories about war and its aftermath inevitably focus on men: the soldiers, the returning veterans, the statesmen. I wanted to know what war was like for those who had been left behind: the women who managed to keep going even as their world fell apart. War reshapes women's lives and often unexpectedly forces them— unprepared—into the role of breadwinner. Charged with their family's survival, they invent ways to provide for their children and communities. But their stories are rarely told. We're far more accustomed to—and comfortable with—seeing women portrayed as victims of war who deserve our sympathy rather than as resilient survivors who demand our respect. I was determined to change this.

So I came to Kabul in search of that story. The plight of Afghan women had won worldwide attention in the wake of the Taliban's ouster by American and Afghan forces, which followed the terrorist attacks of September 11, 2001. I was eager to see what kinds of companies women were starting in a country that had barred them from schools and offices just four years earlier. I brought with me from Boston four pages, single spaced and neatly stapled, containing the names and email addresses of possible sources, the product of weeks of conversations with TV reporters, print journalists, Harvard contacts, and aid workers in the region.

I discussed interview ideas with Mohamad. Over cups of tea in the empty dining room of a hotel frequented by journalists, I asked him whether he knew any women who were running their own businesses. He laughed. "You know that men in Afghanistan don't get involved in women's work." But after a moment of thought he looked up at me and admitted that yes, he had heard there were a few women in Kabul who had started their own companies. I hoped he was right.

As the days passed, I worked my way down the roster of potential interviewees but kept coming up empty. Many of the women whose names I had been given were running nongovernmental organizations, or NGOs, that were not businesses at all. In fact, I was told, when the international community first entered Afghanistan en masse in 2002, it was easier to register an NGO than a company. The incentives were fixed early on. American officials in Washington and Kabul may have been championing Afghan businesswomen, holding public events and spending millions of government dollars on their behalf, but here I was struggling to find a single entrepreneur with a viable business plan. Surely they were out there and I just hadn't looked in the right places?

My deadline was approaching, and I was beginning to fear that I'd return home empty-handed and let down both the *Financial Times* and my professor at Harvard. And then finally a woman who worked with the New York nonprofit organization Bpeace told me about Kamila Sidiqi, a young dressmaker turned serial entrepreneur. Not only did she run her own firm, I was told, but she had gotten her unlikely start in business as a teenager during the Taliban era.

At last I felt a jolt of reporter's excitement, the thrilling rush of news adrenaline that journalists live for. The idea of a burqa-clad breadwinner starting a business under the nose of the Taliban was remarkable for sure. Like most foreigners, I had imagined Afghan women during the Taliban years as silent—and passive—prisoners waiting out their prolonged house arrest. I was fascinated, and eager to learn more.

The more I dug around, the more I realized that Kamila was only one of many young women who had worked throughout years of the Taliban regime. Driven by the need to earn money for their families and loved ones when Kabul's economy collapsed under the weight of war and mismanagement, they turned small openings into large opportunities and invented ways around the rules. As women throughout the world always had, they found a way forward for the sake of their families. They learned how to work the system and even how to thrive within it.

Some staffed foreign NGOs, often in the area of women's health, which organizations the Taliban permitted to continue. Doctors could still work. And so could women who helped other women to learn basic hygiene and sanitation practices. Some taught in underground schools, leading courses for girls and women in everything from Microsoft Windows to math and Dari, as well as the Holy Q'uran. These study sessions took place across Kabul in private homes or, even better, in women's hospitals, the one safe zone the Taliban permitted. But the women could never fully let their guard down; classes would pack up at a moment's notice after someone came running down a hallway to warn that the Taliban were coming. Still others, like Kamila, launched home businesses and risked their safety to find buyers for the goods they produced. Though their vocations differed, these women shared one thing in common: their work meant the difference between survival and starvation for their families. And they did it on their own.

No one had fully told these heroines' stories. There were moving diaries that captured the brutality and despair of women's lives under the Taliban, and inspiring books about women who created new opportunities after the Taliban had been forced into retreat. But this story was different: it was about Afghan women who supported one another when the world outside had forgotten them. They helped themselves and their communities with no help from beyond their poor and broken country, and they reshaped their own future in the process.

Kamila is one of these young women, and if you judge by the enduring impact her work has had on modern-day Afghanistan, it's fair to say that she's among the most visionary. Her story tells us much about the country to which we continue to send our troops nearly a decade after the Taliban's foot soldiers stopped patrolling the streets outside her front door. And it offers a guide as we watch to see whether the past decade of modest progress will turn out to have been a new beginning for Afghan women or an aberration that disappears when the foreigners do.

Deciding to write about Kamila was easy. Actually doing so was not. Security went to pieces during the years I spent interviewing Kamila's family, friends, and colleagues. Suicide bombings and rocket attacks terrorized the city with increasing frequency—and potency. Eventually these grew sophisticated and coordinated enough to pin Kabulis down in their homes and offices for hours at a time. Even the usually stoic Mohamad occasionally showed his nervousness, bringing me his wife's black Iranian-style headscarf to help me look more "local." After each incident I would call my husband to say that everything was okay, and urge him not to pay too much attention to all the bad news in his "Afghanistan" Google Alert. Meanwhile, all across Kabul cement walls rose higher and the barbed wire surrounding them grew thicker. I and everyone else in Kabul learned to live with heavily armed guards and multiple security searches each time we entered a building. Thugs and insurgents began kidnapping foreign journalists and aid workers from their homes and cars, sometimes for cash and sometimes for politics. Journalist friends and I spent hours trading rumors we had heard of attacks and potential attacks, and texting one another when security alerts warned of neighborhoods we should avoid that day. One afternoon following an intense day of interviews I received a worried call from the U.S. Embassy asking if I was the American writer who had been abducted the day before. I assured them I was not.

This worsening reality complicated my work. Afghan girls who worked with Kamila during the Taliban era grew more nervous about meeting with me for fear that their families or bosses would shun the attention a foreigner's visit attracted. Others frightened of being overheard by their colleagues refused entirely. "Don't you know the Taliban are coming back?" one young woman asked me in a nervous whisper. She worked for the United Nations at the time, but had just been telling me all about the NGO she worked for during the Taliban. "They hear everything," she said, "and if my husband finds out I talked to you, he will divorce me."

I didn't know how to answer such questions but did everything I could to protect my interview subjects and myself: I dressed even more conservatively than the

Afghan women around me; wore my own headscarves, which I had bought at an Islamic clothing store in Ana-heim, California; and learned to speak Dari. When I arrived at stores and offices for interviews, I stayed silent for as long as possible and let Mohamad speak to the security guards and receptionists on my behalf. I knew that the better I blended in, the safer we all would be.

One of my reporting trips coincided with an audacious early morning attack on a UN guesthouse that killed five UN workers. For many nights afterward I would jump out of bed and leap into my slippers whenever I heard the neighbor's cat walking across the plastic sheeting that insulated our roof—I thought the noise was someone trying to break in. A friend suggested, only half jokingly, that I keep an AK-47 in my room to defend our house against would-be attackers. I agreed immediately, but my roommates worried that, given my limited fire-arms experience, this would create more danger than it prevented.

Kamila and her sisters also feared for my safety.

"Aren't you worried? What does your family say?" Ka-mila's older sister Malika asked. "It is very dangerous here for foreigners right now."

I reminded them all that they had lived through much worse and had never stopped working. Why should I? They tried to protest, but they knew I was right: they had kept going during the Taliban years despite the risks, not just because they had to but because they believed in what they were doing. So did I.

The fact that I stayed in Kabul then—and kept coming back year after year—earned me their respect and strengthened our friendship. And the more I learned about Kamila's family—their commitment to service and education, their desire to make a difference for their country—the more my esteem for them grew. I strove to be worthy of their example.

Over time Kamila's family became part of mine. One of her sisters would help me with my Dari while another made delicious traditional Afghan dinners of rice, cauliflower, and potatoes for her vegetarian guest from America. When I left in the evenings, they always insisted on checking to make sure my car was outside before letting me put my shoes on to leave. We spent afternoons sitting in our stocking feet in the living room drinking tea and snacking on *toot*, dried berries from the north. When we weren't working we swapped stories about husbands and politics and the "situation," as everyone in Kabul euphemistically referred to security. We sang and danced with Kamila's beautiful toddler nieces. And we worried about one another.

What I found in Kabul was a sisterhood unlike any I had seen before, marked by empathy, laughter, courage, curiosity about the world, and above all a passion for work. I saw it the first day I met Kamila: here was a young woman who believed with all her heart that by starting her own business and helping other women to do the same, she could help save her long-troubled country. The journalist in me needed to know: where does such a passion, such a calling, come from? And what does Kamila's story tell us about Afghanistan's future and America's involvement in it?

That is the story I set out to tell. And those are the questions I set out to answer.

# The Dressmaker of Khair Khana

# 1

# The News Arrives
# and
# Everything Changes

Kamila Jan, I'm honored to present you with your certificate."

The small man with graying hair and deeply set wrinkles spoke with pride as he handed the young woman an official-looking document. Kamila took the paper and read:

This is to certify that Kamila Sidiqi has successfully completed her studies at Sayed Jamaluddin Teacher Training Institute.

KABUL, AFGHANISTAN
SEPTEMBER 1996

"Thank you, Agha," Kamila said. A snow-melting smile broke out across her face. She was the second woman in her family to finish Sayed Jamaluddin's two-year course; her older sister Malika had graduated a few years earlier and was now teaching high school in Kabul. Malika, however, had not had the constant shellings and rocket fire of the civil war to contend with as she traveled back and forth to class.

Kamila clasped the treasured document. Her headscarf hung casually and occasionally slipped backward to reveal a few strands of her shoulder-length wavy brown hair. Wide-legged black pants and dark, pointy low heels peeked out from under the hem of her floor-length coat. Kabul's women were known for stretching the sartorial limits of their traditional country, and Kamila was no exception. Until the leaders of the anti-Soviet resistance, the Mujahideen ("holy warriors"), unseated the Moscow-backed government of Dr. Najibullah in 1992, many Kabuli women traveled the cosmopolitan capital in Western clothing, their heads uncovered. But now, only four years later, the Mujahideen defined women's public space and attire far more narrowly, mandating offices separate from men, headscarves, and baggy, modest clothing. Kabul's women, young and old, dressed accordingly, though many—like Kamila—enlivened the rules by tucking a smart pair of shoes under their shapeless black jackets.

It was a far cry from the 1950s and '60s, when fashionable Afghan women glided through the urbane capital in European-style skirt suits and smart matching headscarves. By the 1970s, Kabul University students shocked their more conservative rural countrymen with knee-skimming miniskirts and stylish pumps. Campus protests and political turmoil marked those years of upheaval. But that was all well before Kamila's time: she had been born only two years before the Soviet invasion of Afghanistan in 1979, an occupation that gave rise to a decade-long battle of Afghan resistance waged by the Mujahideen, whose forces ultimately bled the Russians dry. Nearly two decades after the first Russian tank rolled into Afghanistan, Kamila and her friends had yet to experience peace. After the defeated Soviets withdrew the last of their support for the country in 1992, the triumphant Mujahideen commanders began fighting among themselves for control of Kabul. The brutality of the civil war shocked the people of Kabul. Overnight, neighborhood streets turned into frontline positions between competing factions who shot at one another from close range.

Despite the civil war, Kamila's family and tens of thousands of other Kabulis went to school and work as often as they could, even while most of their friends and family fled to safety in neighboring Pakistan and Iran. With her new teaching certificate in hand, Kamila would soon begin her studies at Kabul Pedagogical Institute, a coed university

founded in the early 1980s during the Soviet years of educational reform, which saw the expansion of state institutions. After two years, she would earn a bachelor's degree
and begin her teaching career there in Kabul. She hoped
to become a professor of Dari or perhaps even literature
one day.

Yet despite the years of hard work and her optimistic
plans for the future, no joyful commencement ceremony
would honor Kamila's great achievement. The civil war
had disemboweled the capital's stately architecture and
middle-class neighborhoods, transforming the city into
a collapsed mess of gutted roads, broken water systems,
and crumbling buildings. Rockets launched by warring
commanders regularly arced across Kabul's horizon, falling onto the capital's streets and killing its residents indis-
criminately. Everyday events like graduations had become
too dangerous to even contemplate, let alone attend.

Kamila placed the neatly printed certificate into a
sturdy brown folder and stepped out of the administra-
tor's office, leaving behind a line of young women who
were waiting to receive their diplomas. Walking through a
narrow corridor with floor-to-ceiling windows that over-
looked Sayed Jamaluddin's main entrance, she passed
two women who were absorbed in conversation in the
crowded hallway. She couldn't help overhearing them.

"I hear they are coming today," the first woman said to
her friend.

"My cousin told me they are just outside Kabul," the other answered in a whisper.

Kamila immediately knew who "they" were: the Taliban, whose arrival now felt utterly inevitable. News in the capital traveled at an astoundingly rapid pace via a far-reaching network of extended families that connected the provinces across Afghanistan. Rumors of the arriving regime were rampant, and the word was out that women were in the crosshairs. The harder-to-control, more remote rural regions could sometimes carve out exceptions for their young women, but the Taliban moved quickly to consolidate power in the urban areas. So far they had won every battle.

Kamila stood quietly in the hallway of the school she had fought so hard to attend, despite all the dangers, and listened to her classmates with a feeling of growing unease. She moved closer so she could hear the girls' conversation more clearly.

"You know they shut the schools for girls in Herat," the sharp-nosed brunette said. Her voice was heavy with worry. The Taliban had captured the western city a year earlier. "My sister heard that women can't even leave the house once they take over. And here we thought we had lived through the worst."

"Come, it might not be so bad," answered her friend, taking her hand. "They might actually bring some peace with them, God willing."

Holding her folder tightly with both hands, Kamila hurried downstairs for the long bus ride that would take her to her family's home in the neighborhood of Khair Khana. Only a few months ago she had walked the seven miles after a rocket had landed along the road in Karteh Char, the neighborhood where her school was located, damaging the roof of a hospital for government security forces and knocking out the city's bus service for the entire evening.

Everyone in Kabul had grown accustomed to seeking safety between doorjambs or in basements once they heard the now-familiar shriek of approaching rockets. A year earlier the teacher training institute had moved its classes from Karteh Char, which was regularly pummeled by rocket attacks and mortar fire, to what its director hoped was a safer location in a once-elegant French high school downtown. Not long afterward yet another rocket, this one targeting the nearby Ministry of Interior, landed directly in front of the school's new home.

All these memories raced through Kamila's mind as she boarded the rusty light blue "Millie" bus that was once part of the government-run service and settled into her seat. She leaned against the large mud-flecked window and listened to the women around her while the bus began to maneuver bumpily through Karteh Char's torn-up streets. Everyone had her version of what the new regime would mean for Kabul's residents.

"Maybe they will bring security," said a girl who sat a few rows behind Kamila.

"I don't think so," her friend answered. "I heard on the radio that they don't allow school or anything once they come. No jobs, either. We won't even be able to leave the house unless they say so. Perhaps they will only be here for a few months . . ."

Kamila gazed through the window and tried to tune out the conversations around her. She knew the girl was probably right, but she couldn't bear to think about what it would mean for her and her four younger sisters still living at home. She watched as shopkeepers on the city's dusty streets engaged in the daily routine of closing their grocery stores, photo shops, and bakery stalls. Over the past four years the entrances to Kabul's shops had become a barometer of the day's violence: doors that were wide open meant daily life pushed forward, even if occasionally punctured by the ring of distant rocket fire. But when they were shut in broad daylight, Kabulis knew danger waited nearby and that they, too, would be best served by remaining indoors.

The old bus lurched forward amid a belch of exhaust and finally arrived at Kamila's stop. Khair Khana, a northern suburb of Kabul, was home to a large community of Tajiks, Afghanistan's second-largest ethnic group. Like most Tajik families, Kamila's parents came from the north of the country. The south was traditionally Pashtun terrain. Kamila's father had moved the family to Khair Khana during his last tour of duty as a senior military officer for the Afghan army, in which he had served his country for more than three decades. Kabul, he thought at the time, offered his nine girls the best chance of a good education. And education, he believed, was critical to his children's, his family's, and his country's future.

Kamila hurriedly made her way down the dusty street, holding her scarf over her mouth to keep from inhaling the city's gritty soot. She passed the narrow grocery store fronts and wooden vegetable carts where peddlers sold carrots and potatoes. Smiling, flower-laden brides and grooms stared down at her from a series of wedding pictures that hung from the wall of a photo shop. From the bakery came the delicious smell of fresh naan bread, followed by a butcher shop where large hunks of dark red meat dangled from steel hooks. As she walked Kamila overheard two shopkeepers trading stories of the day. Like all Kabulis who remained in the capital, these men had grown accustomed to watching regimes come and go, and they were quick to sense an impending collapse. The first, a short man with balding hair and deeply set wrinkles, was saying that his cousin had told him Massoud's forces were loading up their trucks and fleeing the capital. The other man shook his head in disbelief.

"We will see what comes next," he said. "Maybe things will get better, Inshallah. But I doubt it."

Commander Ahmad Shah Massoud was the country's defense minister and a Tajik military hero from the Panjshir Valley, not far from Parwan, where Kamila's family came from. During the years of resistance against the Russians, Dr. Najibullah's forces had imprisoned Kamila's father on suspicion of supporting Massoud, who was known as the "Lion of Panjshir" and was among the most famous of the Mujahideen fighters. After the Russians withdrew in 1992, Mr. Sidiqi was freed by forces loyal to Massoud, who was now serving in President Burhanuddin Rabbani's new government. Mr. Sidiqi went to work with Massoud's soldiers in the north for a while, eventually deciding on retirement in Parwan, his boyhood home and a place he loved more than any other in the world.

All through the preceding summer of 1996, Massoud had vowed to stop the Taliban's offensive even as the relentless bombardment of the capital continued and Taliban forces took one city after another. If the government soldiers were really packing up and heading out of Kabul, Kamila thought, the Taliban could not be far behind. She picked up her pace and kept her eyes on the ground. No need to look for trouble. As she approached her green metal gate on the corner of Khair Khana's well-trafficked main road, she sighed in relief. She had never been more grateful to live so close to the bus stop.

The wide green door clanged shut behind Kamila, and her mother, Ruhasva, rushed out into the small courtyard to embrace her daughter. She was a tiny woman with wisps of white hair that framed a kindly, round face. She kissed Kamila on both cheeks and pressed her close. Mrs. Sidiqi had heard the rumors of the Taliban's arrival all morning long, and had been pacing her living room floor for two hours, anxious for her daughter's safety.

Finally home, with her family close and darkness falling, Kamila settled down on a velvety pillow in her living room. She picked up one of her favorite books, a frayed collection of poems, and lit a hurricane lamp with one of the small red and white matchboxes the family kept all over the house for just such a purpose. Power was a luxury; it arrived unpredictably and for only an hour or two a day, if at all, and everyone had learned to adjust to life in the dark. A long night lay before them, and they waited anxiously to see what would happen next. Mr. Sidiqi said little as he joined his daughter on the floor next to the radio to listen to the news from the BBC in London.

Just four miles away, Kamila's older sister Malika was finally winding down a far more eventful day.

❋

"Mommy, I don't feel well," said Hossein.

Four years old, he was Malika's second child and a favorite of his aunt Kamila. She would play with him in the family's parched yard in Khair Khana and together they would count the goats and sheep that sometimes passed by. Today his small body was seized by stomach pain and diarrhea, which had worsened as the afternoon passed. He lay on the living room floor on a bed of pillows that Malika had made in the center of the large red carpet. Hossein breathed heavily as he fell in and out of a fitful sleep.

Malika studied Hossein and wondered how she would manage. She was several months pregnant with her third child and had spent the day inside, heeding a neighbor's early morning warning to stay home from work because the Taliban were coming. Distractedly she sewed pieces of a rayon suit she was making for a neighbor, and watched with growing concern as Hossein's condition worsened. Beads of sweat now covered his forehead, and his arms and legs were clammy. He needed a doctor.

From her closet Malika selected the largest chador, or headscarf, she owned. She took care to cover not just her head but the lower half of her face as well. Like most educated women in Kabul, she usually wore her scarf draped casually over her hair and across her shoulders. But today was different; if the Taliban really were on their way to Kabul they would be demanding that women be entirely covered in the full-length burqa, known in Dari as a chadri; it concealed not just the head but the entire face. Already this was the rule in Herat and Jalalabad, which had fallen to the Taliban just a few weeks earlier. Since she had no burqa, the oversize veil was the closest

Malika could come to following Taliban rules. It would have to suffice.

Once her sister-in-law had arrived from the apartment upstairs to look after her older boy, Malika gathered Hossein in her arms and tucked him inside her baggy black overcoat. Holding him close to her swelling belly, she hurried out the door for the ten-minute walk to the doctor's office.

The silence in the street frightened Malika. At this early afternoon hour her neighborhood was usually crowded with a jumble of taxis, bicycles, donkeys, and trucks, but today the streets were empty. The rumors of the approaching army had sent her neighbors deep into their homes, behind their gates and window coverings. It was now a waiting game, and no one knew what the next few days would bring.

Malika winced at the sound of her own heels clacking on the sidewalk. She focused her eyes on the ground as she struggled to hold the wide folds of her scarf in place, but the heavy fabric kept slipping off her head, forcing her to juggle and shift the small boy in her arms as she performed the awkward dance of replacing the shawl, keeping the child covered, and walking as quickly as she could. An afternoon shadow began to fall on Karteh Parwan's uneven rows of homes and shops.

Finally Malika made a right turn off the main road and reached an office that occupied the ground floor of a shabby strip of storefronts, all of which shared the same cement floors and low ceilings. Several rows of brown stone separated the shops from the balconied apartments above. Relieved to be inside and to rest for a moment, Malika checked in with the doctor, who had come out of his examining room when he heard the front door.

"My son has a fever; I think he may be very sick," she said. "I brought him here as soon as I could."

The doctor, an older gentleman whom her husband's family had visited for years, offered her a kind smile.

"No problem, just take a seat. It won't be long."

Malika settled Hossein into a wooden chair in the dark and empty waiting room. She walked the floor, trying to calm herself, then rubbed her belly for a moment and inhaled deeply. Little Hossein was pale and his eyes looked glassy and expressionless. She wrapped her arms tightly around him and pulled him closer to her.

Suddenly a noise on the street outside startled her. Malika jumped from her chair toward the window. Gray clouds hovered over the street and it had grown dark outside. The first thing she could make out was a shiny dark truck. It looked new, certainly newer than most cars in Kabul. And then she saw three men standing beside the pickup. They wore turbans wrapped high and thick and carried long rods in their hands that looked like batons. They were striking at something or someone, that much she could tell.

With a start Malika realized that the figure huddled in front of them was a woman. She lay in the middle of the street, crouched in a ball, and was trying to fend off the blows. But the men would not stop. Malika heard the dreadful slapping sound of the wooden batons as they hit the helpless woman—on her back, her legs, over and over again.

"Where is your chadri?" one of the men shouted at his victim as he lifted his arms above his head to strike her. "Why are you not covered? What kind of woman are you to go out like this?"

"Stop," the woman pleaded. "Please have mercy. I am wearing a scarf. I don't have a chadri. We never had to wear them before!"

She began to sob. Malika's eyes teared as she watched. Her instincts commanded her to run into the street and rescue this poor woman from her attackers. But her rational mind knew it was impossible. If she left the doctor's office she would be beaten as well. These men would have no problem hitting a pregnant woman, she thought. And she had a sick child to protect. So she stood helplessly by the window listening to the woman cry, and wiped her own tears away.

"You think this is the last regime?" one of the young men shouted. His eyes were black with kohl, the night-colored cosmetic that Taliban soldiers wore. "This is not Dr. Najibullah or the Mujahideen," he said, his club hitting her once more. "We believe in sharia, Islamic law, and this is now the law of the land. Women must be covered. This is your warning."

Finally the men got back in their truck and left. The woman bent over unsteadily to grab her handbag from the street and slowly limped away.

Malika turned back to Hossein, who was folded up in his chair and moaning softly. Her hands shook as she held his small fingers. Like the woman outside, she was from a generation of Kabul women who had never known life under the chadri. They had grown up in the capital long after Prime Minister Mohammad Daoud Khan had embraced the voluntary unveiling of his countrywomen in the 1950s. King Amanullah Khan had attempted this reform unsuccessfully thirty years earlier, but it wasn't until 1959, when the prime minister's own wife appeared at a national independence day celebration wearing a headscarf rather than the full chadri, that the change finally took hold. That one gesture stunned the crowd and marked a cultural turning point in the capital. Kabul's next generation of women had gone on to become teachers, factory workers, doctors, and civil servants; they went to work with their heads loosely covered and their faces exposed. Before today many had never had reason to wear or even own the full veils of their grandmothers' generation.

Suddenly the tide had turned again. Women would

now be forced to dress in a style—and assume a way of life—they had never known, by rulers who had known nothing else. Was this what was in store for her, too, once she left the doctor's office? Malika felt her heart pounding in her chest as she wondered how she was going to get Hossein and herself safely home. Like the woman's outside, Malika's scarf was large, but it was hardly big enough to cover her whole face and convince the soldiers of her piety. She held Hossein tightly, trying to comfort herself as much as her son.

Just then the doctor returned.

After a quick but thorough examination he assured Malika that it was nothing serious. He prescribed plenty of fluids and gave her a prescription to fill, then walked Malika and Hossein back to the waiting room. When they reached the front door Malika stopped.

"Doctor, I wonder if we could stay here for a few more minutes?" She pointed her chin down in the direction of the little boy in her arms. "I need to rest for just a moment before carrying him home again."

Malika didn't want to talk about what she had just seen, but it weighed heavily on her mind. She needed to a make a plan to get them safely out of this situation.

"Of course," the doctor replied. "Stay as long as you wish."

Malika paced the waiting room floor and prayed for help. She could not go back out onto the street without a chadri, that much was certain. But she had no idea how she would get hold of one.

Suddenly her heart leapt. Through the window she saw Soraya, her older son's elementary school teacher, walking down the street toward the doctor's office. Malika recognized the purposeful gait from a distance and then glimpsed the teacher's face peeking out from beneath her dark scarf. A small grocery sack dangled from each arm. Malika ran toward the door. After she had scanned the sidewalk to make certain the Taliban were no longer in sight, she took a furtive step out of the doctor's office.

"Soraya Jan," she called from the doorway. "It is Malika, Saeed's mother."

The startled teacher hurried over and Malika related what she had seen in the street.

Soraya shook her head in amazement. She had spent the past hour buying what vegetables she could for her family's evening meal of pilau, Afghan aromatic rice, and naan bread, but food had become hard to find these days. A Taliban blockade now strangled the city, preventing trucks carrying food from reaching the capital's 1.2 million residents. Today Soraya had barely managed to get hold of a few potatoes and some onions. The market had been abuzz with rumors of the Taliban's arrival, but Malika was the first person she knew who had actually seen the capital's new soldiers up close.

"My house is just around the corner," Soraya told

Malika, taking her hand. "You and Hossein will come with me, and we'll figure out how to get you a chadri to wear home. Don't worry; we'll find a way."

Malika smiled for the first time all day.

"Thank you, Soraya Jan," she said. "I am so grateful."

The women quickly walked the one block to Soraya's house, which stood behind a bright yellow gate. They didn't speak a word during the short trip, and Malika wondered if Soraya was praying as hard as she was that they wouldn't be stopped. She couldn't get the image of the woman in the street off her mind.

A few minutes later they sat together in Soraya's small kitchen. Malika tightly gripped a glass of hot green tea and relaxed for the first time in hours. She was deeply thankful for the warmth of her friend's home and the fact that Hossein, who had taken a pill at the doctor's office, was already feeling a bit better.

"I have a plan, Malika," Soraya announced. She called for her son, Muhammad, who was in the other room. Once the little boy appeared, Soraya gave him his mission. "I need you to go to your aunt Orzala's house. Tell her we need to borrow one of her chadri for Auntie Malika; tell her we will return it to her in just a few days. This is very important. Okay?"

The eight-year-old nodded.

Just half an hour later young Muhammad bounded into the living room and solemnly handed Malika a white plastic shopping bag; the handles had been carefully tied together and inside was a blue chadri. "My aunt says you can borrow the chadri as long as you need it," Muhammad said, beaming.

Malika unfolded the fabric, which was really several panels of material that had been sewn together by hand. The front section, about a yard in length, was made of a light polyester with a finely embroidered border at the bottom and a cap at the top. The chadri's longer side and back panels formed an uninterrupted wave of intricate and meticulously pressed accordion pleats that hung close to the floor. Wearing the garment required getting underneath the billowy folds and making certain the cap was in just the right spot for maximum visibility through the webbed eye slit, which turned the world slightly blue.

The family invited Malika to stay for dinner, and after sharing a plate of rice and potatoes by candlelight on the living room floor, she stood up and put on the chadri. The hem of her fashionable brown suit pants stuck out from beneath the veil. Malika had worn the covering only a few times before when visiting family in the provinces, and she now found it tricky to maneuver among the slippery pleats and panels. She struggled to see out through the small eye vent, which was just two inches long and three and a half inches wide. She tripped over the fabric while saying her last good-byes to Soraya's family.

"One of my sons will bring the chadri back to you soon," Malika said, embracing her friend and rescuer.

She took Hossein by the hand and began to walk home under the starry evening sky, stepping slowly and carefully to make certain she didn't trip again. She prayed the rockets would wait for her to make it back safely.

Days would pass before she would see her family in Khair Khana and share her harrowing story. Malika, it turned out, was among the first to experience what lay ahead for them all. It would be just as the young woman at Sayed Jamaluddin had predicted.

# 2

# A Time of Good-byes

The radio hummed static from its perch on the living room shelf. Kamila's father, Woja Abdul Sidiqi, placed his ears against the old Chinese machine's black speakers and tried to decipher the BBC reporter's words. An imposing man with a shock of white hair and an angular, nearly regal visage, Mr. Sidiqi revealed his army roots in his military posture and serious demeanor. The children looked on silently; no one ever dared interrupt this somber evening ritual. He gingerly adjusted the aging machine's dials and soon the living room was filled with the sound of the BBC's Persian news service broadcast live from London. The evening program, always a staple of Mr. Sidiqi's dinnertime routine, had now become the family's main link to the outside world.

Dramatic bulletins had arrived over the radio in the month since the bearded, turbaned young Taliban troops rolled into Kabul in heavy tanks and shiny Japanese pickup trucks, euphoric in what they claimed was their divine triumph. On the first morning they hanged the communist former president, Dr. Najibullah, from a red and white striped traffic post in Ariana Square, right in the center of downtown Kabul. Since he was loathed for his close ties to the godless Soviets and his crackdown on Islamist figures during the 1980s, the Taliban put his assassination on grisly display for all the world to see. They dangled cigarettes from the former president's lifeless mouth and stuffed his pants pockets with money to symbolize his moral bankruptcy. His battered and swollen corpse languished for two days at the end of a rope.

Mr. Sidiqi had been recruited to the army as a teenager in the 1960s by a government official who had come to visit his home province of Parwan. He saw a great deal of political turmoil in his military career as an artilleryman, topographer, and senior adviser, including the 1973 overthrow of the sitting king, Mohammed Zahir Shah, by his former prime minister Mohammad Daoud Khan. Daoud dissolved the monarchy and declared the country a republic, but five years later he was murdered by an educated group of communist hard-liners who routinely imprisoned, tortured, and killed their opponents. The Soviet Union became convinced that the revolutionaries they once supported could no longer be trusted, and in

1979 the Red Army invaded. Afghanistan had been at war ever since.

Each of the governments Mr. Sidiqi served had faced a near-constant threat of overthrow from rivals both within and without, and all relied on the army to maintain stability. But today a vastly different military force was in control, and their tactics were very new and very public. Crowds of boys and men piled into the busy intersection at Ariana Square to see for themselves the murder of Dr. Najibullah, and they reported home to their wives, sisters, and mothers the extraordinary scene they had witnessed. The message could not be mistaken: a new regime was in charge.

Kamila's father worried about what would happen to his own family now that he could see how the Taliban would deal with its enemies. He had, after all, served under Dr. Najibullah and worked with Massoud, the Panjshiri fighter who had become the Taliban's biggest foe and still commanded enough forces to stop them from controlling the entire country. But Mr. Sidiqi urged his daughters not to be concerned. "I'm just an old retiree; I've got nothing at all to do with politics," he reassured them. As the days passed, however, Kamila grew more uneasy. The Taliban began harassing young Tajik men, rounding them up from mosques and bazaars on suspicion of providing arms and information to Massoud's forces, which were now making a stand north of Kabul. Taliban soldiers with Kalashnikovs slung over their shoulders patrolled the city in their tanks and trucks, looking to stamp out trouble and crush any opposition.

Mr. Sidiqi, an educated man who had traveled the country during his army days and believed that ethnic differences should not matter to Afghans, struggled to explain to his daughters why these men had ample reason to fear the world beyond their refugee camps. Many of them were orphans whose parents had been killed when Soviet bombs laid waste to their southern villages. The Russian invasion, he said, had taken these soldiers' families and their homes. They had never gotten to know their country, or its capital. "I think this is the first a lot of these boys have seen of Kabul," he told the girls, "and probably the first time they've seen so many people from so many different backgrounds." Most had grown up in refugee camps in the southern and eastern regions of Pakistan. What little grounding they had in their own history had come through the filter of barely educated, deeply religious madrassa teachers who schooled them in a singular, unforgiving interpretation of Islam very different from the Afghan tradition. In the camps in which they had grown up, many refugee families kept their wives and daughters indoors nearly all the time to ensure their safety and honor. "These young men who serve under the Taliban's white flag have had almost no contact with women during their entire lives," Mr. Sidiqi told his daughters.

Indeed, their training had taught them to avoid exposure to the amoral temptation of the other sex, whose rightful place was at home behind closed doors. This made the life and culture of the urban capital appear even more foreign and bewildering to the young soldiers who were now in charge of its streets. Through their eyes, Kabul looked like a modern-day Sodom and Gomorrah where women roamed freely and alone, wearing seductive makeup and Western-style clothing; where storekeepers did not faithfully heed the call to prayer; where excesses thrived and alcohol was plentiful. Kabul to these zealous young men was a sinful city full of crime and debauchery and desperately in need of spiritual cleansing.

Kabulis watched helplessly as the Taliban began reshaping the cosmopolitan capital according to their utopian vision of seventh-century Islam. Almost immediately they instituted a brutal—and effective—system of law and order. Accused thieves had one hand and one foot cut off, and their severed limbs were hung from posts on street corners as a warning to others. Overnight, crime in the monumentally lawless city dropped to almost zero. Then they banned everything they regarded as a distraction from the duty of worship: music, long a part of Afghan culture, and movies, television, card playing, the game of chess, and even kite flying, the popular Friday afternoon pastime. And they didn't stop at actions alone: creating a representation of the human figure was soon forbidden, as was wearing European clothing or haircuts. After a short grace period to grow them, the length of men's beards could be no shorter than the distance made by a clenched fist. Shaving was prohibited. Modernity, and anything associated with it, had been sentenced to banishment.

But of all the changes the Taliban brought, the most painful and demoralizing were the ones that would fundamentally transform the lives of Kamila, her sisters, and all the women in their city. The newly issued edicts commanded:

Women will stay at home
Women are not permitted to work
Women must wear the chadri in public

Women had been officially banned from schools and offices, though many teachers, including Kamila's older sister Malika, went to work each week to pick up paychecks for jobs they could no longer do. Girls' schools were quickly shuttered; in twenty-four hours the student body of Sayed Jamaluddin leapt from 20 percent to 100 percent male. And the chadri became mandatory, no exceptions allowed. For many women, however, including Kamila and her four sisters, the clothing restrictions were the least of their problems. The worst was that they had no place left to go; they had been banished to their living rooms. Overnight, women vanished from the streets of a city where only days before they had accounted for nearly 40 percent of civil servants and more than half of all teachers. The impact was immediate and devastating, particularly for the thirty thousand Kabul families that were said to be headed by widows. Many of these women had lost their husbands during the endless years of war, first with the Soviets and then with their own countrymen. Now they couldn't even work to support their children.

For Mr. Sidiqi, the longtime patriot and loyal public servant, the situation was especially distressing. As a young man, he had worked in a state-of-the-art $25 million Swiss textile mill in his hometown of Gulbahar. He had watched the European women working alongside their husbands and Afghan colleagues. All that separated these women who had jobs and an income from those in his own family was education, a reality he would never forget. Through all the war and upheaval he witnessed during his long army career, Mr. Sidiqi was determined that all of his children—the nine girls as well as the two boys—enjoy the privilege of school. He would not distinguish between his sons and daughters when it came to the duties of the classroom. As he often told the eleven of them, "I look on all of you with one eye." To him it was his highest obligation and a duty of his faith to educate his children so that they could share their knowledge and serve their communities. Now he watched with a sinking heart as the Taliban closed girls' schools and forced women inside.

Gathered around the radio, the Sidiqi family sat together listening to the Taliban's statements on Radio Afghanistan—recently renamed Radio Sharia by the city's new governors—and grew ever more despondent. Each night new rules came through the machine. We don't have much of anything left to take away, Kamila thought to herself one night before abandoning all her worries to the comfort of sleep. How many more rules can there be?

None of the girls had left the house since the Taliban took Kabul, and they were convinced they couldn't bear much more confinement. For seven days straight the young women had roamed from room to room reading their favorite, and then their less-favorite, books, tuning in to the news quietly, so no one outside could hear, telling stories to one another and listening to their parents discuss the family's next move. Never before had any of the girls lived for this long within the confines of their courtyard. They knew that many conservative families in the country's rural regions, particularly its south, practiced purdah, the isolation of women from all men except their nearest relatives, but such rules were totally foreign to them. Mr. Sidiqi and his wife had encouraged each of their nine daughters to become a professional, and so far the three oldest had become teachers. The younger girls, who ranged in age from six to seventeen, were still studying and preparing for university. "The pen is stronger than the sword," Mr. Sidiqi would remind his children while they pored over their books in the evenings. "Keep studying!"

And now, day after dreary day, these energetic, educated girls sat around in their bare feet on pillows in the living room listening to events unfold over the BBC, wondering how long life could continue like this. All of their plans for the future had simply disappeared in what felt like a heartbeat.

Kamila tried to be optimistic. "I'm sure it won't be more than a few months," she'd say to her sisters when they grew restless and began to snap at each other. But privately she was sick at heart. She ached for her old life, which had been filled with school and friends. And she found it painful to imagine the world outside going on uninterrupted without her or any of Kabul's women. Surely this could not last forever. Yes, she would wear the chadri, but she could not stay indoors with nothing but empty time for much longer; there had to be a way to study or to work, even if the university remained off-limits. There were five girls at home in Khair Khana, and Kamila knew that her father and brother couldn't support them all forever. If this went on much longer, she would have to find a way to help.

But the reports of life on Kabul's streets remained grim. Kamila's brother Najeeb described to his sisters in detail a city that had been transformed. It was true, most stores had reopened, and more food could be found in the markets now that the Taliban blockade had at last been lifted. Prices had even fallen a little since the roads into Kabul had reopened. You could sense the relief in the air now that the fighting had finally subsided and rockets no longer fell on the city each day. Security had instantly improved. But the capital was eerily quiet. Traffic no longer jammed the city's roads. And almost no women could be found on the streets. The two that Najeeb did see one afternoon walked quickly beneath full chadri and kept their heads down.

And something else was new on Kabul's streets: the patrols of the Amr bil-Maroof wa Nahi al Munkir, the Ministry for the Promotion of Virtue and Suppression of Vice, which had been styled after a similar ministry in Saudi Arabia, one of the few countries that supported the Taliban. Fanning out across the city, the Amr bil Maroof assumed the role of "chief enforcers of moral purity." Just the name Amr bil-Maroof was now enough to frighten men and women alike. These passionate foot soldiers energetically enforced the Taliban's unique interpretation of Pashtunwali-influenced sharia, or Islamic law. They performed their tasks with a zeal and a severity that even their leaders in Kandahar sometimes found dreadful.

Many of them were barely old enough to grow a beard and wore no uniform, just white or black turbans and shabby *shalwar kameez*, a baggy knee-length shirt and loose-fitting pants, sometimes covered by a vest. They carried *shaloqs*, the wooden batons that had so terrified Malika that day in front of the doctor's office, as well as metal antennas and leather whips. At the time of prayer the Amr bil-Maroof's men put their whips to work corralling shopkeepers and yelled at their brothers to "close their stores and come to the mosque." They patrolled the streets day and night looking for rule-breakers, especially women. If a woman dared to pull back her chadri to steal a look at something she wanted to buy at the market, or if a wrist accidentally slipped out while she crossed an intersection, a member of the Amr bil-Maroof would appear from nowhere to apply swift and brutal "justice," right there for all to see. Rarely did a man come to the rescue of a woman who was being beaten; everyone knew he would be next if he tried to help. The Talibs hauled their worst offenders, including women accused of infidelity, off to prison, a black hole from which only time and sometimes, for lesser crimes, family money could—occasionally—free them.

Kamila's neighbors began to leave Kabul as the crackdown grew more severe. But it was not just politics driving them out: it was the quickly collapsing economy. Money dried up and families found themselves forced to live on nearly nothing. The government now paid its tens of thousands of civil servants only occasionally, if at all, and families with working wives, sisters, and daughters had all lost at least one income. Long before the Taliban arrived many in Khair Khana had fled the indiscriminate killing and violence of the civil war. Those who stayed behind had sold almost everything they owned to survive the fighting, including the doors and windows of their houses, which could be turned into firewood. Now most of the dwindling middle class that still lived in Khair Khana and had the means to leave had decided to pack up and make the risky journey to Pakistan or Iran.

So it was no surprise when Najeeb arrived home from the market one evening to announce that his cousins and their family were leaving town. A tall boy with a handsome face and a young man's confidence, Najeeb spoke in a tone of barely concealed urgency.

"I've just been to see Uncle Shahid and he says they can't stay here any longer. The girls can't study and they're worried about what will happen to the boys." Kamila had never seen her even-tempered brother so upset. Her cousins were also teenage boys who, like Najeeb, faced increasing danger on the streets of Kabul simply because they were Tajiks from the north. With each week the risks they faced got worse, not better, as their families had hoped at the beginning.

In different times Kamila's relatives would have come to tell her father their plans in person, over several glasses of home-brewed chai and a silver tray filled with almonds, pistachios, and *toot*, the dried berry snack. But today families were leaving the city quietly and quickly, while they could. They had no time to tell anyone, even those they loved and trusted most.

Kamila had overheard her parents discussing their options several days before, and she knew it was unlikely that Mr. Sidiqi would join her mother's family in Pakistan or Iran. It was simply too dangerous to risk the journey with five young girls in tow. To get to Pakistan they would have to travel from Kabul through Jalalabad to the Torkham border, then, if the crossing gate were closed, hire a man to smuggle them over the mountains. After that they would need to find a taxi or bus to take them into one of the cities, most likely Peshawar, where tens of thousands of Afghans had already settled, many in refugee camps. Bandits lined the narrow passes along the rugged terrain, and rumors abounded of girls being abducted along the way. Besides, who knew what would happen to the Khair Khana home Mr. Sidiqi had worked so hard to build if they abandoned it? Everyone knew it was impossible to get property back once you had left it. Within weeks some family that was desperate for shelter would move in and take both the house and the land, and when the family returned to Kabul Mr. Sidiqi would be stuck in court for years trying to get his home back. If he had to leave, that would be one thing, but whatever you could say about the Taliban, they had made the city safer. For the first time in years Kabulis could sleep with their doors open if they wished. As long as his five girls at home followed the rules of the new regime, they would be fine. And they would be in their own country.

But for the men in Kamila's family, the danger grew hard to ignore. It was no use insisting that Mr. Sidiqi was no longer in the military or was apolitical, or that he was clearly too old to be fighting for the opposition. The Taliban had begun combing neighborhoods house by house trying to uncover pockets of resistance that remained in the restive and now largely subdued capital. The young soldiers were searching for fighting-age men, a term broad enough to include any male who could potentially present a threat to the Taliban regime, beginning with teenagers. The Taliban accused men belonging to the Uzbek, Hazara, and Tajik ethnic minorities of backing their opposition, including Massoud, whose forces had now regrouped in the Panjshir Valley in hopes of drawing the Taliban northward to continue their fight on more favorable terrain. At seventeen, Najeeb and his cousins had become prey for mass detentions. Once they were picked up, the Taliban could press-gang them into service and ship them off to fight. Neighbors' sons had been questioned on the street by Talibs and forced to show their identification cards. If the young men hailed from the north they faced the threat of immediate detention in the Taliban jails that had sprung up all across Kabul.

Each time Najeeb left the house, Kamila's mother feared he wouldn't return. Every day now he came home with a story about some friend or neighbor who was heading abroad to find work, amid promises to send money home to the family as soon as he could. As able-bodied men poured out of Kabul it became more and more a city of women and children who had been left behind with no one to support them and no way to support themselves.

It was only a matter of time before security fears forced the Sidiqi men to follow their friends and neighbors out of Kabul. They halfheartedly made plans for Eid ul-Fitr, the festival that celebrated the end of the holy month of Ramadan, but by the end of the sixth week of Taliban rule, the decision could no longer be delayed: the family would have to separate. Otherwise, the men could end up in prison or on the front lines.

Sitting in the pale hurricane lamp light of the living room, Mr. Sidiqi shared his plan with his seven children. He would leave immediately for Gulbahar, his hometown forty-five miles north in Parwan. Growing up, the older children had regularly made the two-hour trip to see relatives and enjoy family picnics near the Panjshir River, whose cool waters ran just behind the Sidiqis' house on fertile land that Kamila's grandfather had farmed. They had passed many summer Fridays playing by the water and running about in the sprawling outdoors that was greener and more vast than anything they ever knew in

Kabul. These idyllic family outings ended with the arrival of the Russians in Afghanistan and the war of resistance that took hold in the north. In eight successive offensives the Soviet tanks had destroyed much of the region's farmland and its way of life, but they would never make lasting gains here in Massoud's stronghold. Massoud's forces were far more determined to protect their homeland than the Russians ever were to conquer it, and his fighters used guerrilla tactics and Parwan's treacherous terrain to maintain their advantage. Once the Soviets withdrew and the Mujahideen took power in 1992, the younger Sidiqi children got to know Gulbahar's mud huts, clear streams, and lush fields. Though much had been destroyed in the fighting, all the children had come to love their village's leafy quiet and its stunning views of the distant Hindu Kush mountains. Now, with yet another war under way, Kamila wondered how much more Gulbahar would have to endure.

Even though the fighting had moved north from Kabul into Parwan province, Mr. Sidiqi believed he would be safer there than in the capital. He would send for Kamila's mother once he had settled in and assessed the situation. Meanwhile Najeeb would look after the women until the family could decide on the young man's next move. Kamila and her sisters didn't have to ask why they couldn't accompany their father to the north, for they already knew why he would refuse: it was too dangerous to travel with five young women through Taliban and then Northern Alliance territory. But Mr. Sidiqi had another, unspoken, reason: he worried that in the north his girls would be besieged by wedding proposals, which would be awkward to continually rebuff. Kamila's father didn't intend to be inhospitable to would-be suitors, and he was by no means against marriage for his daughters, but he wanted them first to have the chance to complete their studies and then work if they chose to. For this they were much better off in Kabul. The girls must now find a way to read and learn as much as they could, and be ready to return to school once the Taliban eased their rules.

The night before he left, the girls worked with their mother to prepare food for his journey, stuffing plastic shopping bags with thick piles of naan bread and dried fruit. When they had finished, and the younger girls had settled down to read by lamplight, Kamila sat with her father in a corner of the living room. His lean figure towered over her, as he commanded her, quietly, solemnly, to be strong and to help her mother. "They all need you, the girls especially, and I am counting on you to guide them, and to be their example." Kamila held back her tears. "I don't think this will be over soon; it may even take years. But I am sure you will be a good leader for your sisters. And I know you will make me proud, just as you always have."

All night long Kamila thought of his words. He was

counting on her. And so were her sisters. She had to find a way to take care of her family.

Kamila did not weep as she bid her father good-bye the next morning. Neither did her mother, who had been up most of the night readying his things. The family had already seen so much fighting and war in the past decade; even the little ones knew better than to wish things were otherwise. The Taliban were settling into the city for the long run, establishing a government, holding press conferences, and demanding permission to take the country's seat at the United Nations. All Kamila and her sisters could do now was learn to make their way under the new order.

# 3

## Stitching the Future Back Together

"What are you reading?" Kamila asked, looking over her shoulder at her sister Saaman, who had stretched out across the deep red woven carpet on the living room floor. Khair Khana had had no power for several days, and shadows from the hurricane lamp fluttered against the room's bare walls.

Saaman was lost in thought. Her book of poems lay open in front of her, but she had long ago abandoned it; she was far too distracted to concentrate. The sound of Kamila's voice jolted her back to the quiet evening. A pretty teenager with fine features and a perfectly symmetrical face, Saaman was more serious and more reserved than her gregarious older sister. She possessed a quiet grace that manifested itself as shyness when she met someone for the first time.

"Some of your Maulana Jalalludin," replied Saaman. After a moment she sighed: "Again."

She rolled onto the other side of her pillow, adjusted her ponytail, and tried to focus on her poetry once more.

Only months before, Saaman had passed the competitive college entrance exams, known in Afghanistan by their French name, *concours*, and had won a coveted seat at Kabul University. Her parents had been immensely proud of their sixth-born daughter, who would be the first in the family to enter the country's oldest and most respected university. She had just begun her first semester of study in the science department and was reveling in university life. Then the Taliban took Kabul. Saaman was trying to bear the abrupt end to her education with composure, but she found it difficult to accept being forced to trade her classroom for a living room filled with half a dozen restless girls.

She was hardly the only young woman in Kabul trying to fill her days. Across the capital, women of all ages and backgrounds were learning to make do in a city run by men who wanted them to disappear. The Taliban had dug in for the winter and perhaps much longer; no one dared to guess. Meanwhile, fighting ground on between the new regime and Massoud's forces, and the United Nations pecked away at a peace process that lacked even the energy to stall.

Months had passed since the Taliban's arrival, and the girls in Kamila's house no longer spoke of a swift end to their home detention. Instead they watched helplessly as the nine men of the Taliban High Court issued edicts that strengthened the rules of their banishment and regulated ever smaller details of their everyday lives. Walking in the middle of the street was now prohibited, as was wearing high-heeled shoes. Clothing must be baggy and loose-fitting "to prevent the seditious limbs from being noticed," and chadri could not be made from any lightweight material through which arms or legs might be seen. Mixing with strangers and going out without a *mahram*, or male relative, had been outlawed.

Kamila and her sisters banded together to seek relief from the creeping despair that threatened to suffocate them. And they began to think about possible solutions. "We should ask Habiba Jan to bring some of her books over," Kamila said to Saaman one morning while they finished cleaning the kitchen after a breakfast of hot chai and toasted naan. Habiba's family lived only two houses down the road, making visits fairly safe, even with the current restrictions.

"I'm so sick of reading the same thing over and over again. Maybe we could share some books with our friends." She was on a roll.

"Yes, yes, what a great idea," Saaman replied as she dried her hands on a rag. "We should also talk to Razia.

She reads a lot, though I'm not sure what kinds of books she likes. We have the poetry covered; maybe she can bring some of those great Persian detective stories—I think she's addicted to them." Saaman felt energized for the first time in weeks.

With that conversation began the girls' semiregular neighborhood book swap. Every few days a handful of girls from the northeast section of Khair Khana would stop by the Sidiqi home to drop off books they had fin-ished and pick up new ones. Everyone was excited by the hunt for new volumes to share with the group, and as they cycled through their own small libraries they reached out to borrow from family collections. Kamila's sitting room became an informal trading floor, with books lined up along the wall, spines out and organized alphabetically by author in neat rows for easy browsing. Girls from the neighborhood came by every day, and they all sat together in a circle, snacking on chai and pistachios and sharing their passion for the authors they loved, egging each other on to read their favorites.

Both Kamila and Saaman loved the famous Persian poets. A copy of Maulana Jalalludin Mohammad Balkhi-Rumi's classic *Divani Shamsi Tabrizi*, an epic poem of forty-five thousand Dari verses, floated constantly between the sitting room and the girls' sleeping chambers down the hall. The thirteenth-century poet, a native of the north-eastern province of Balkh and known to most Western-

ers simply as Rumi, defined the Islamic mystical Sufi
tradition in which meditations on music and poetry bring
man nearer to God and the presence of the divine. Another writer who deeply moved the girls was the lyric poet
Hafez, born in 1315 in the southern Iranian city of Shiraz.
Hafez wrote ghazals, or odes, that chronicled human loss
and sought comfort in the immense beauty of God's divine
love and creation. The girls took turns reading the stanzas
aloud:

*from* POEMS FROM THE DIVAN OF HAFIZ

*translated by Gertrude Lowthian Bell*

The breath of Dawn's musk-strewing wind shall blow,
The ancient world shall turn to youth again,
And other wines from out Spring's chalice flow;
Wine-red, the judas-tree shall set before
The pure white jessamine a brimming cup,
And wind flowers lift their scarlet chalice up
For the star-pale narcissus to adore.

The long-drawn tyranny of grief shall pass,
Parting shall end in meeting, the lament
Of the sad bird that sang "Alas, alas!"
Shall reach the rose in her red-curtained tent.

. . .

Dear is the rose—now, now her sweets proclaim,
While yet the purple petals blush and blow;
Hither adown the path of Spring she came,
And by the path of Autumn she will go.
Now, while we listen, Minstrel, tune thy lay!
Thyself hast said: "The Present steals away;
The Future comes, and bringing—what? Dost know?"

The lines from their treasured Persian literary heritage took the girls far away from the Taliban's rigid idea of Islam, which grew out of a different tradition, the Deobandi, which strenuously opposed mysticism and rejected music and dance as corrupting influences. The Deobandi tradition began in northern India as a reaction to the injustices of colonial rule and evolved over time to embrace only the most literal and puritanical interpretations of Islam.

The book swap distracted the girls for several weeks, but as much as she enjoyed reading and sharing paperbacks with her friends, Kamila found herself growing more and more restless. Even the new supply of books was becoming dull, as she devoured each one, then read it again. How long can I just sit here? she thought. She knew there were women who had found ways to work; she had heard rumors about a few teachers who were running schools in their houses, for example, but the political situation remained so unpredictable that most women thought it wiser to stay indoors until something changed.

And things would have to change. There were too many widows who needed to support themselves and their families, and too many girls who were hungry for education. Frustration was growing as the economy imploded under a yoke of mismanagement, war, and neglect. Foreign aid, in the form of subsidized wheat distributions, had become critical to helping Kabul feed itself. The whole city now qualified as "vulnerable" in the aid vernacular. The situation was quickly becoming unbearable.

Kamila's family was fortunate. Her father had stashed away some savings from his army salary and rent he received each month for a nearby apartment he owned. The money would not support the large family at home indefinitely, but it had been enough to hold them over until Mr. Sidiqi could figure out another option.

If Kamila's mother was worried about their situation, she didn't show it; nor did she share her concerns with her oldest daughter. But Kamila watched with great anxiety as the large family's resources grew thinner. Her brothers, Rahim and Najeeb, went shopping less frequently and brought home fewer groceries and supplies at one time. Meat had become an even greater luxury. Kamila wondered how long the money that remained could last, given how many of them it had to feed.

To make matters worse, the family had heard nothing

from Mr. Sidiqi since he left Kabul weeks earlier. Few homes had telephones. There was no national mail system—illiteracy ran rampant in the largely rural country—and the ongoing fighting had badly damaged the makeshift communications systems that had managed to survive the Soviet invasion. A thriving network of family and friends stepped in to fill this vacuum; scores of people who regularly traveled back and forth between Kabul and the north served as impromptu postmen, transmitting messages between loved ones and sharing news with those who had been left behind. Kamila's mother tried not to worry and comforted herself with the knowledge that her husband had survived two of his country's wars already. But she felt uneasy being so far from him at such a precarious time. They had shared three decades and eleven children, and his safe arrival in Parwan was her only wish. She planned to join him there as soon as he sent word that the situation was secure enough for her to come.

The Taliban, meanwhile, had taken their fight to the north. They followed Massoud to his stronghold in the Panjshir Valley and attacked General Abdul Rashid Dostum's forces in the northern city of Mazar-e-Sharif, home of the legendary Blue Mosque. They were determined to eliminate their remaining opponents and consolidate control over the entire country. Then the world would have no choice but to recognize the Taliban as Afghanistan's rightful and legitimate government and bestow upon the men from Kandahar all the benefits of nationhood, including foreign aid and the United Nations seat that they so desperately coveted.

While they were fighting their own countrymen, the Taliban were also battling for control of the economic resources of the agriculturally fertile and mineral-rich north, which would give them the industrial base they lacked in the south. Nearly two decades earlier, the Soviets had spent millions of dollars developing the region's vast energy resources for their own benefit. Crude oil, iron reserves, and coal could all be found in abundance in the northern territories, which had for years received Kabul aid dollars as a reward for being easier to govern than the restive south.

Back in Kabul, the economy worsened, and families slipped from poor to truly destitute. The Taliban pushed back against the international aid community's focus on what the men from Kandahar called the "two percent of women" who worked in Kabul's offices. They issued more edicts, cloaked in the language of diplomacy:

"We kindly request all our Afghan sisters to not apply for any job in foreign agencies and they also should not go there. Otherwise, if they were chased, threatened, and investigated by us, the responsibility will be on them. We declare to all foreign agencies to respect the issued regulation of Islamic State of Afghanistan and strictly avoid employment of Afghan female staff."

They continued to beat women in the streets, including beggars who extended their worn, cracked hands to passersby in hope of a handout. Taliban soldiers thrashed them with their *shaloqs* and berated them for being outside without a *mahram*. They ignored the fact that a shortage of men at home was the reason most of these women were forced onto the streets in the first place. Stories were spreading of those who had turned to prostitution to support their children, a situation that carried both great shame and danger for the women and their families. But for many there was no alternative. If caught, they faced public execution.

Kamila heard about everything that was happening outside on the streets from her brothers, who faithfully served as her eyes and ears, but she saw little of it for herself. She ventured out only rarely, and when she did leave the safety of her house, she remained strictly within the limits of Khair Khana. The farthest she had dared to go were the shops of the nearby Lycée Myriam bazaar—named for its proximity to Lycée Myriam high school—where she could find everything from food to fabric, including the required and now-ubiquitous chadri. None of the women Kamila saw moving through Lycée Myriam's narrow maze of stalls and stores were begging; they were simply buying what they needed as quickly as possible while trying to avoid the roaming caravans of the Amr bil-Maroof, who would punish them simply for talking too loudly or wearing clothing that rustled. Even if women hadn't felt so nervous and harried by the ever-present Taliban soldiers, there was no point in lingering to browse since they couldn't see much of anything through the rectangular mesh of their chadri. Laughing in public was also prohibited, but there seemed little risk of breaking that rule these days. In Kabul, all the joy had gone out of shopping as well.

Interaction between male shopkeepers and their female customers was closely monitored. Women kept their conversation to a minimum as they picked out and paid for their goods. Even asking after family, as polite Afghan society demanded, could create suspicion and attract Taliban attention. Male tailors could no longer measure women for dresses, since this could lead to immoral thoughts and was a violation of the Taliban's complete segregation of men and women who were unrelated by family or marriage.

Walking through the Lycée Myriam bazaar, Kamila noticed other changes in her favorite stores. Gone was the cheerful music and the pictures of Indian film stars. Even the catalog photos of smiling women modeling pricey Pakistani dresses had vanished from the walls of the tailoring shops. And hardly any fancy dresses remained in the boutiques; with the economy imploding, women hiding in their homes, and wealthy Kabulis fleeing by the hour, the market for expensive and elaborate imported frocks had simply dried up.

Kabul was now a different city. The problems of the Mujahideen period had been grave, but the city had never been so abandoned and stripped of hope.

As winter set in, the city's plight worsened. Costs for staples such as flour and oil climbed higher each month, and for most families just getting by was becoming more and more of a challenge. Kamila's mother made sure her seven children had all the basics of food and clothing, but like everyone around them, their household was only barely functioning. Kamila felt the tremendous pressure that weighed on her family, and she spent hours each day trying to think of ways she could help. She felt certain that things could not continue this way, with eight people depending on the small income from the rental apartment and their dwindling savings. Along with food, they needed books and school supplies for Rahim, the only one of the children who could still attend class. They also had to buy wood for the squat *bukhari* stove that heated the sitting room and oil for the hurricane lamps. Najeeb, the older of the two boys, was in the best position to help the family, but as things worsened his safety was more and more at risk. And besides, there were no jobs left in Kabul.

It wasn't long before Najeeb and his mother decided he would have to leave for Pakistan with several other young men whose families the Sidiqis knew. If he couldn't find work there he would go to Iran and would send his salary home to the women as soon as he could. But it was impossible to know when that would be. Already tens of thousands of refugees had headed across the border. Kamila and her sisters heard countless stories of the difficulties they faced finding jobs and places to live. Most were stuck in massive, crowded refugee camps where families competed for assistance from an overburdened aid community that struggled to provide health care, schools, and work programs.

The Sidiqi family needed help now. If only she could come up with a plan that would allow her to earn money while staying within the Taliban's rules, Kamila thought, she could take the pressure off Najeeb and her father. She felt just how much her family needed her, and knew she had to find a way to do her part. Dr. Maryam, who rented the Sidiqis' apartment and used it as an office, had managed to do just that; she was a doctor who was still able to practice medicine, despite the restrictions. As long as no men entered her office and all her patients were female, her clinic had no problems from the Taliban.

This is what I have to figure out, Kamila thought to herself. I need to find something I can do at home, behind closed doors. I need to find something that people need, something useful that they'll want to buy. She knew she had very few options. Only basic necessities mattered now; no one had money for anything else. Teaching school might be an option, but it was unlikely to earn her enough money, since most families still kept their girls at home out of fear for their safety. And she certainly didn't want her income to depend on an improvement in the security situation.

Kamila spent long days thinking about her options, considering which skills she could learn quickly that would also bring in enough afghani to make a difference for her family. And then it came to her, inspired by her older sister Malika, who, along with being a great teacher, had over many years developed into a talented—and sought-after—seamstress. Women from her neighborhood in Karteh Parwan loved her work so much that Malika's tailoring income now earned her almost as much as her teacher's salary. That's it, Kamila thought. I'll become a seamstress.

There were many positives: she could do the work in her living room, her sisters could help, and, most important of all, she had seen for herself at Lycée Myriam that the market for clothing remained strong. Even with the Taliban in power and the economy collapsing, women would still need simple dresses. As long as she kept quiet and didn't attract unnecessary attention, the risks should be manageable.

Kamila faced just one major obstacle: she had no idea how to sew. Until now she had been focused on her books and her studies and had never shown any interest in sewing, even though her mother was an expert tailor, having learned from her own mother when she was growing up in the north. Mrs. Sidiqi had made all of her own clothing as a teenager, and she in turn had taught Malika when the young woman was struggling with her first high school sewing assignment. Now that the Taliban had barred women from classrooms, Malika was again considering becoming a full-time tailor, particularly since her husband's transport business had slowed considerably under the new regime.

"Malika," Kamila whispered to herself. "Surely she will teach me. And no one is as talented as she is. . . ."

A few days later Kamila set off for Malika's house in Karteh Parwan, making her way in her chadri toward the bus stop under the late morning sun. She hadn't been able to send word ahead to her sister to expect her visit, but these days there was little risk of finding Malika or any of her other older sisters away from home; life had moved indoors. Since Rahim was in school Kamila went by herself, unaccompanied by a *mahram*, and her heart pounded as she walked all alone the few hundred yards to the corner. The city looked like it had been evacuated. Kamila kept her head down and prayed that no one would notice her.

Fortunately, she had to endure only a short wait before the aging blue and white bus lumbered down the street and shuddered to a stop. Kamila quickly noticed that, like everything else in Kabul, there was something different about the vehicle. She was no longer allowed use the front door, as she always had, but was forced to enter through a door toward the rear, into a new women's section. An old *patoo*, a woolen blanket that often doubled as a covering for men, hung unevenly from a white rope and managed to hide the women in the back from the men who sat up front with the driver. As she boarded the bus, a young boy took Kamila's fare in his palm; children his age were the only males who were still permitted to have contact with women outside their family.

As the bus pulled out of Khair Khana's main road, Kamila gazed out the window. She could see almost no cars and very few people, mainly men who were huddled together in the cold trying to sell whatever their family still owned. Their wares lay sprawled out on ratty blankets on the side of the street: rubber tubes from old bicycles, unkempt baby dolls, worn shoes without laces, plastic jugs, pots and pans, and stacks of used clothing. Anything they had that they thought others might value. Armed Mujahideen no longer manned the checkpoint at the traffic circle that marked the end of her neighborhood and the beginning of Khwaja Bughra; instead, groups of Kalashnikov-wielding Taliban guarded the intersection.

Inside the bus the women spoke in hushed tones of Kabul's growing desperation.

"Things have never been so bad for us," one woman said. Kamila could see nothing of their faces; all she had were voices, which sounded slightly muffled from behind the chadri. "I don't know what we will do. My husband lost his job and my girls are home with me. Perhaps we'll go to Pakistan, but who knows if things will be any better there."

A woman sitting opposite answered in a quiet voice, shaking her head from side to side while she spoke. She sounded exhausted.

"You know, my husband has left for Iran and now I fear they'll try to send my son to the front lines. What will happen to my children? There's no one left to help us. It has become so difficult."

Kamila listened as the women shared their troubles. At last, about fifteen minutes later, the bus arrived in Karteh Parwan.

Stepping onto the street, she walked down Karteh Parwan's main boulevard until she arrived at Malika's narrow lane. Once there she exhaled fully for the first time since she left Khair Khana. She hadn't realized how nervous she had been. After passing row on row of one- and two-story houses she finally reached Malika's, a white, squat, two-family home. Malika and her husband lived on the first floor and her brother-in-law's family lived above them.

Kamila knocked on the wooden door, and in only a few moments she found herself in her older sister's warm and powerful embrace. Kamila felt a rush of relief as she stepped inside the living room she knew so well.

"Come in, come in, I'm so glad you're here. This is a

surprise!" Malika said as she kissed her sister on each cheek. Her belly had gotten so much bigger; Kamila realized that the baby must be due soon. "Did you have any problems on the way? I've heard the patrols are very strict now. You have to be so careful when you go out."

"Oh, no, it was fine," Kamila said, dismissing her fears of just a minute earlier. No need to make Malika worry more than she already did. Her oldest sibling had been like a parent to the younger children in the large Sidiqi brood; she had helped to raise all seven of her younger sisters, feeding them and getting them ready for school every day, since their mother had her hands full with eleven children, a husband, and a household to run. "There were a lot of women on the bus. Everyone was talking about how hard things are."

The two women sat down to steaming glasses of freshly made chai and a plate of nuts and butter cookies. Kamila filled Malika in on all that was happening at home, including Najeeb's imminent departure and her own worries about their finances. Then, after a moment's silence, Kamila came to the point of her visit.

"Malika Jan," she said. "I need your help."

She recounted to her sister how she had explored every idea she could think of to make money for the family, how she wanted to find a way to support them, to make things easier for their father and mother.

"Malika, I think that if I knew how to sew I could start

making dresses at home and perhaps I could sell them to the shops at Lycée Myriam."

Malika listened intently as her sister spoke.

"Would you teach me?" Kamila finally asked.

Malika sat silently as she weighed the idea. She, too, had been hearing of women who, out of sight of the Amr bil-Maroof and interfering neighbors, sewed dresses or knitted blankets in their living rooms to earn money for their families. Necessity was turning these women into entrepreneurs. With no jobs available and no employers willing to hire them, they were making their own way, creating businesses that would help them feed their children.

Malika worried about her sister taking such risks, but she knew the family needed the income. It was the best option Kamila had.

"Yes, of course I'll help," she said. "I'm sure you'll learn quickly; you always have, ever since you were little!"

But there were conditions.

"You have to follow my rules, Kamila. Number one: never go out alone, as you did today. You have to bring Najeeb or someone else with you. And you can't ever be on the streets during the time of prayer—that's when soldiers are patrolling the shops and it will be very dangerous."

Kamila listened, nodding at everything she said.

"No talking to strangers, ever, including women, because you never know who might be listening. Or who might want to turn someone else in for their own reasons. And most of all, you can't ever be seen speaking with any men other than one of our brothers, particularly shop-keepers. You have to assume that the Taliban are always watching, that you are never invisible. You just have to be watchful every second you're outside, okay?"

"Definitely," Kamila said. "You're right. You know I wanted to bring one of our brothers with me today but they were both very busy. I promise I'll do everything you say and will be extremely careful from here on out."

Malika looked at her, unconvinced. She wasn't sure her strong-willed sister had ever stopped to think about the consequences once she set her mind on something.

"Really, I promise you," Kamila said, seeing her sister's hesitation. "I don't want to break the rules or cause prob-lems for anyone; I just need to work for our family. And Malika, I am going mad with nothing to do. I have to be useful again."

Malika realized that it would be pointless to stand in her sister's way, no matter how worried she was. She could tell by Kamila's tone of absolute certainty that she had al-ready decided to go forward with her plan anyway—with or without her help.

"Well, then," Malika said, putting down her tea and removing the snacks from the wooden table. She moved like a woman with no time to waste. "Let's begin."

Kamila followed her sister into her sewing area, which

was just off the living room. Malika had carved out this small workspace a few years earlier, and it had become her own private refuge, a corner of quiet amid the noise and laughter of her two boys. Partially completed dresses and a dark pair of women's trousers hung here and there from chairs and table corners. Malika was in the middle of making a pantsuit for a neighbor, she explained.

Three small machines stood at attention on the sewing table. Malika used one to hem clothing, particularly garments that were made from thick fabric. Another was for embroidery. But the device she turned to most often was her "zigzag," a lightweight beige-colored machine that could make more than a dozen kinds of stitches and was powered by a black pedal that sat beneath it on the floor.

Reaching for a swath of powder blue rayon fabric that was leaning against the wall, Malika began to explain to Kamila how to make a simple dress with beading.

"First, you begin by cutting the fabric," she said.

As she continued, Malika grabbed a pair of fabric shears from a nearby shelf that was filled with sewing supplies—measuring tape, needles, dozens of spools of colored thread. A dusty shaft of afternoon sunlight streamed into the sitting room from the courtyard, glancing off the metal scissors. Malika carefully maneuvered a smooth, straight line against the material she was cutting.

She picked up a plastic stencil in the shape of a flower

from her worktable and held it against the top corner of the cut fabric. With a thin marker she outlined the shape of the petals, tilting the fabric to show Kamila what she was doing. Then she stuck a small silver needle through the neat and even holes of the stencil to puncture the fabric beneath. Beading would later fill these small spaces.

Malika was a natural teacher. She explained each step to her sister in detail as she went, demonstrating her technique in slow and deliberate moves. Her attentive pupil followed the lesson closely, and took over where she could in the hope that doing it herself would help her better remember everything Malika was showing her. "Now I wish I had paid better attention when Mother taught you to sew, Malika Jan!" she exclaimed.

Soon Kamila was ready to bead. Together she and her sister sewed the tiny, hollow stones onto the flower by hand until the dress had a yellow blossom with small spaces of blue at its center.

Malika then turned back to finishing the garment, and announced that Kamila was ready to learn how to use her cherished zigzag. Malika showed her how to thread the machine, and how to properly, and comfortably, position herself in the chair. In only a few minutes Kamila was moving the pedal expertly.

"See? You're a very good student, just as I expected," Malika exclaimed, as together they worked on the final seams of the pantsuit. Kamila smiled and shared a laugh with her sister; after three hours of intense focus she was finally relaxed. It felt great to be working again, and she was so excited to be learning a skill that could very well become the lifeline she needed. Malika ended her sister's first training session by showing her how to complete the hems at the bottom of the skirt and sleeves. When the machine's staccato finally stopped, they had an elegant blue dress with a beaded flower near the neckline that would be smart enough for any occasion, including their cousin's upcoming Kabul wedding. Kamila felt proud of her work and—she confessed only to herself—was somewhat amazed that she had helped make such a pretty garment.

But there was little time for the sisters to enjoy their success; the afternoon had passed quickly and evening would soon arrive. Malika gently folded the new dress into a plastic bag while Kamila secured her chadri. With a curfew in effect they had to get Kamila to the bus stop soon to make certain she would be back in Khair Khana long before dark. Without a *mahram*, Kamila faced an even greater chance of being stopped. The sooner she was home, the better.

"Malika, thank you so much for all your help," Kamila said as she hugged her older sister good-bye in the doorway she had been so grateful to reach just a few hours earlier. "You always take such good care of all of us."

Malika reached behind her for a folded piece of white paper, which she handed to Kamila. Inside lay a thick pile of colorful afghani.

"This should be enough to help you buy fabric and materials to get started," Malika said.

Kamila embraced her tightly. The money was an incredibly generous gift at such a time.

"I will repay you as soon as I can. I promise it won't be long," she told her sister.

On the bus home, Kamila held her black plastic bag closely to her, beneath her chadri. Inside was the folded blue dress, the first piece of clothing she had ever made. She couldn't wait to show Saaman and the others when she got home.

As she bounded into her house, grateful for Allah's protection, Kamila heard the sounds of her sisters' lively chatter coming from the sitting room. Their mother sat smiling with them.

Kamila had arrived just in time to hear the good news.

At last they had received word from Mr. Sidiqi; a cousin who had just returned from Parwan had passed his letter on to Najeeb. The note was written on worn, thin paper that was already turning yellow.

*Thanks be to Allah, I have arrived in Parwan. The fighting continues, but I am well. I will soon see you here, Inshallah.*

Kamila watched her mother's eyes well up as she read her the letter, and she saw the release of a worry that had gone unspoken for so long. Mrs. Sidiqi folded the letter into fours once more and placed it on the low wooden table in their living room. Then she returned to the family's dinner. Soon she would leave for Parwan, with Najeeb beginning his journey to Pakistan not long afterward.

# 4

# The Plan Goes
# to Market

O h, this is so pretty," Saaman proclaimed as she held
the blue dress in her hands and marveled at Kamila's work. "I just love it, especially the beading."
And then: "What are you going to do with it?"

"I am going to sell it," Kamila answered with a big
smile. "Tomorrow I'll take it to the Lycée Myriam bazaar
to show the tailors there what we can do. I'm going to see
if we can get some orders from one of the shops there."

"Why you? And why there?" Saaman asked. Her
dark brown eyes grew larger as her imagination con-
jured the worst possible scenarios. "Can't someone else
sell it for you? You know what things are like now; you
could be beaten or taken to jail just for leaving the house
at the wrong time. Who knows what could happen, and

with father no longer here to help if something goes wrong . . ."

Saaman's voice trailed off as she halfheartedly waited for her sister's answer, but she knew what was coming. Everyone in the family knew that Kamila was not easily moved; her strong will and determination were famous among the Sidiqi clan. Once she had committed herself to an idea she wouldn't let go, regardless of the danger. Sayed Jamaluddin was a perfect example: Her older sisters had pleaded with her to stay home from school during the civil war years while rockets regularly fell on Kabul. It simply wasn't safe to go to class. But Kamila had insisted it was her duty to her family to finish her studies and that her faith would help to protect her. In the end, she won her father's blessing to remain in school, unlike so many other girls whose studies were cut short by war. After all, he was the one who had taught her that learning was the key to the future—both her own and her country's.

As Saaman expected, Kamila had no intention of backing down from her plan, but she promised she would take all the precautions Malika had insisted on: She would stay out of Lycée Myriam during prayer time and she wouldn't speak to anyone she didn't know. She would take Rahim as her *mahram*. Anyway, she asked her sisters, if she didn't go, who would? Her work would help her family, which was a sacred obligation of Islam.

And she firmly believed her faith would protect her and keep her safe.

There was no arguing with Kamila. Instead, Saaman buried her concern beneath a litany of questions.

"Where will you start?" she asked. "Maybe you could try Omar's tailoring store inside the bazaar? Or maybe it would be better to try the one we usually go to along the main strip of shops, where we know people?"

"I don't know yet. We'll have to see how it goes," Kamila responded, trying to seem unfazed by the risks she faced as she launched the second stage of her new venture: finding shops that would do business with her. "I'll start with one or two of the stores inside the bazaar; maybe they'll be interested. I'm sure someone will. Look how lovely this dress is!"

Kamila held the garment up to her shoulders as she spoke. For just a moment she allowed her imagination to run, envisioning the woman who might wear it someday for a special occasion. But she quickly forced herself back to the matter at hand.

"Malika told me that if we can get some steady orders from a shop she'll help us with more designs," Kamila said, folding the blue dress once more and carefully returning it to the plastic bag that lay next to her on the living room floor where they all sat. "We can build a dressmaking empire, the Sidiqi Sisters!" she added, enjoying the sound of it.

"Kamila Jan, I know you know what you're doing, but

please . . ." Laila, the youngest of the girls in the room, had been quietly listening to the conversation. She regarded her sisters with a mix of awe and fear; at fifteen, she was long accustomed to hearing the older girls discuss their plans, but the risks they faced had never seemed so formidable—or so close to home. The Mujahideen years had been dangerous for certain, but back then the violence had struck at random. Today everyone knew the risks that waited just outside their front door; what was harder to anticipate were the consequences. If Kamila got caught speaking to a shopkeeper she could be simply yelled at, or taken into the street and beaten, or, worst of all, she could be detained. It all depended on who saw her. And then where would they all be? Kamila was the oldest, and right now she was responsible for her remaining brother and four sisters at home.

Najeeb had left the house in Khair Khana two weeks earlier on a sunny winter morning. He carried only a small vinyl overnight bag with a few changes of clothing and some toiletries; he could find whatever else he needed in Pakistan, and he didn't want to risk losing anything he valued during the journey there. He left his books in his room and told Kamila to put them to good use while he was away.

"Everything will be just where you left it when you return," Kamila promised. She struggled against her tears. She wanted so badly to be strong for her brother.

He promised to write as soon as he had settled in Pakistan.

Then a knock came at the front door. It was time to go.

Kamila walked him out through the courtyard they had played in together for so many years. He stopped for a moment before he unlatched the metal slide.

"Kamila, take care of everyone, okay?" Najeeb said. "I know it's a lot for you, but Father wouldn't have left you in charge if he didn't think you could manage. I'll send help soon, just as soon as I can."

Faced with her brother's departure, Kamila at last gave in to her tears. She just couldn't bear the idea of Najeeb going out into the world without her. How much danger would the young man face before she saw him again? And when would that be? Months? Years?

She stood at the gate hugging Najeeb good-bye.

"God keep you safe," she said quietly as she at last let him go and took a step back from the door so he could pass. She wiped the tears from her cheeks and tried to muster a reassuring smile. "We'll be fine here. Don't worry about us."

At last the gate slammed shut and he was gone. The young women stood huddled together, staring wordlessly at the green door.

Kamila realized she really was in charge now, and she had to act like it.

"Okay, then," she said, turning to her sisters and leading the girls back inside, "whose turn is it to make lunch?" That afternoon, without Najeeb's good cheer and their mother's comforting words to help pass the hours, Kamila realized how desperately the girls needed something else to focus on. They didn't just need income; they needed a purpose. She simply had to make a success of her dressmaking business.

❄

The next morning was cloudy and quiet as Kamila and Rahim set out for the mile-and-a-half journey to Lycée Myriam. The blue dress lay in folded squares at the bottom of the black carry-all Kamila held tightly at her side. Under her chadri Kamila wore a large, dark tunic, ground-skimming baggy pants, and low rubber-heeled shoes. She wanted to give the Taliban no reason to notice her during this short trip. Her pulse raced and her heart crashed against her chadri with unshakable intensity.

With Najeeb gone, it now fell to Rahim to serve as his sisters' eyes and ears. Though only thirteen, he had suddenly become the man of their house, and the only person in the Sidiqi household who could move around the city freely. Today he was serving as Kamila's *mahram*, the chaperone whose presence would help keep her out of trouble with the Taliban.

Rahim walked close to his sister past the shops and stores along Khair Khana's main road. The two spoke little as they walked toward the market. Soon Kamila spotted a few Taliban soldiers patrolling the sidewalk ahead of them, and she quickly realized they would be better off using the back roads of the neighborhood they knew so well. She and Rahim still had the hometown advantage; the Taliban, most of whom came from the south, remained strangers to the capital. It wasn't unusual for traffic all over the city to be turned on its head by soldiers who drove their tanks and pickup trucks the wrong way down one-way roads, sometimes at high speed. Though they governed Kabul, they still did not know it.

Kamila guided her younger brother through the winding, muddy side streets that led to Lycée Myriam. He felt responsible for keeping his sister safe, especially now that his father and older brother were gone, and he tried to stay a few steps in front of her so that he could see what lay ahead. He still found it terribly strange to behold Kamila in full chadri; he confessed that he couldn't imagine how she could see the road in front of her through the tiny latticed window of her veil. Biting cold and fear kept their pace quick and purposeful.

Kamila didn't allow herself to think about the many things that could go wrong; instead she kept her mind trained on the work ahead as they passed rows of houses along cramped streets that were clotted with dirt and mud. She had not shared the reason for their unusual trip with Rahim, wanting to protect him in the event they were stopped. She would tell him later, as they got closer. In a different time her black tote bag would have been loaded full of schoolbooks, but today it contained a hand-made dress that she hoped would be the start of her new business.

After half an hour Kamila and Rahim arrived at the outskirts of Lycée Myriam. Through her chadri Kamila could make out the bubbling chaos of wooden vegetable carts, clothing stalls, and faded brown storefronts. Most of Khair Khana knew that a handful of the street-front shops doubled as photo and video stores, but these busi-nesses had been officially outlawed by the Taliban, so there was no sign of the underground enterprises they hid behind copy machines and grocery counters. The smell of cooking meat floated through the air as they approached the sprawling bazaar, which stretched north for nearly half a mile. Kamila glanced around at a few stalls that sold shoes and suitcases, then shared her plan with her brother.

"Don't say anything, Rahim," she cautioned him. "Let me do the talking. If the Taliban come, and if there are any problems, just tell them you are accompanying me as we do our family's shopping, and we will be heading home as soon as we're done." Rahim nodded. Assuming the role of bodyguard and caretaker, the young man did not stray very far from his sister's side. He looked right and left every few steps, watching for any sign of trouble. Together the siblings walked into the covered section of Lycée Myriam, a giant indoor shopping mall that was filled with stands and small shops that sold all manner of goods, often in unwieldy piles haphazardly perched on tables and shelves: women's clothes, men's *shalwar kameez*, linens for the home, stacks of chadri, and even children's toys. It was a bewildering maze that first-time visitors found nearly impossible to navigate. Kamila looked around and noticed a few women coming and going from the stalls that sold shoes and dresses. She couldn't tell whether she knew any of them, since none of these women were recognizable except by their shoes. Turning left, she walked toward a small storefront just off the bazaar's main walkway; there she found one of the dress shops she and her sisters had frequented for years. Through the open door she saw a burly shopkeeper manning the counter. He had a clear view of the corridor outside and would be able to spot most of what was happening along the walkway that connected other shops to his. This would be helpful, Kamila thought, in the event the Amr bil-Maroof, the feared "Vice and Virtue forces," came by while she was inside.

Pausing for a moment, Kamila waited in the doorway until a woman at the counter paid for her dress and left. Then she entered the shop with a strong, purposeful stride, hoping her nervousness would be undetectable beneath her show of confidence. She knelt down and pretended to examine a stack of dresses that were folded in tidy squares behind a glass case; together they made a cheerful rainbow of colors.

"Can I help you, miss?" the shopkeeper asked. He was a broad-shouldered man with curly dark hair and a bulging paunch. Kamila noticed that his eyes were fixed on two things at once: his front door and his customer.

"Thank you, sir," Kamila said, speaking in a firm but quiet tone as she stood up to answer him. She checked to make certain Rahim was next to her. "Actually, I'm a tailor and my sisters and I make dresses. I have brought a sample of our work to show you. Perhaps you would be interested in placing an order?"

Before he could reply she reached into her bag and neatly spread the blue dress across the glass counter. Her hands trembled, but she worked deftly. She pointed to the beading. "It is very nice for weddings or for Eid," she said. Her heart beat in her ears, and she leaned against the counter to steady herself.

The shopkeeper picked up the dress and began to inspect it more closely. Suddenly a large, blue-clad figure Kamila saw out of the corner of her eye approached the counter. The shopkeeper dropped Kamila's blue fabric in a heap on the glass but to his—and Kamila's—relief it turned out to be just another female shopper with her *mahram*. Kamila struggled to look busy while she waited.

She didn't dare to look at her brother; she was sure he was as nervous as she was. *What have I gotten us into by coming here?* she thought to herself. *I am always so full of ideas, but maybe I should have thought this one through a bit more. . . .*

But at last the woman departed, and the shopkeeper returned.

"Another seamstress like you came to see me earlier this week," he said, speaking in a low voice. "She also offered to make dresses for my store. I've never really bought much from local women before, but I think I am going to have to start now. Things are tough for everyone, and no one can afford the imported clothes anymore."

Kamila felt a small surge of excitement. As she had seen during her last trip to Lycée Myriam, most shopkeepers no longer thought it worth making the risky trip to Pakistan for a handful of dresses that only a few Kabulis could buy. This was her opportunity.

"Okay, I will take it," he said, putting Kamila's sample next to another pile of dresses on his side of the glass. "Can you make more like this? I don't need so many dresses, actually, but I could use some more *shalwar kameez* for women, simpler clothing that people use for every day."

"Oh, yes, that will not be a problem," Kamila said. She kept her voice quiet and even so as not to betray the wave of elation she felt. And she felt grateful for the anonymity of her chadri. "We can produce as much as you need."

The storekeeper returned the smile he could not see. "Very good. Then I will take five pantsuits and three dresses. Can you have them ready by next week?"

Kamila assured him she could. The store owner then took down bolts of polyester blends and rayon in different colors from a shelf behind him. Picking up his scissors, he cut enough material to make the suits he had ordered and placed the fabric into a dark shopping bag that he handed to Rahim. Throughout their short exchange Kamila saw that he had been keeping a close watch on the doorway for any sign of the Amr bil-Maroof. He had no desire to be caught speaking with a female customer, even if her *mahram* was present. So far things had been uneventful.

"Okay, then, I will see you in a week," he said. "I am Mehrab. What is your name so that I can know you when you come back?" Now that everyone had to wear the chadri, all his customers looked the same.

Where her answer came from, Kamila did not know. But as soon as the shop owner had spoken she realized it was too dangerous to use her real name.

"Roya," Kamila said. "My name is Roya."

Picking up her black carry-all from the counter, Kamila thanked Mehrab and promised she would return the following week. She and Rahim left the store and made their way back toward the street. Though the entire transaction had taken less than fifteen minutes, Kamila felt as if hours had passed.

Walking back into the gray morning, Kamila was nearly bursting with excitement. She felt that she was at the beginning of something important, something that could change their lives for the better. She fervently hoped so, but she admonished herself to stay focused. "No need to get ahead of myself when there is so much work to be done. Let's just get the first order finished right. No more big ideas until then."

"Come, let's go home and tell the girls!"

Throughout the visit with the storekeeper Rahim had stood still as a tree, watching his sister protectively. Even when Mehrab had placed his order, Rahim had been careful to show no emotion. He didn't want to give anyone a reason to look more closely at the transaction that was taking place inside the shop. Now that they were outside he beamed at his older sister and congratulated her on getting her first order. He was very proud of her work.

"I was so surprised when you told him to call you Roya," he said. "That was the only time I almost slipped and laughed! You are really a good saleswoman, Kamila Jan."

Kamila laughed softly beneath her chadri.

"And you are a very good *mahram*," she said. "Mother would be proud."

She kept them moving at a steady pace, for they needed to be far from Lycée Myriam by the time they heard the call to prayer.

Kamila felt invigorated; for the first time since the Taliban's arrival four months earlier she had something to look forward to. And something to work for. She walked back toward the house with a bounce in her gait as Rahim marveled out loud at his sister's new name. "Roya," he said. "Roya Jan." He practiced saying it again, trying to get used to it, just as he had gotten used to being the only boy in a house full of girls, all of whom now depended on him for nearly everything they needed from the outside world.

As they walked, Kamila contemplated the long list of supplies she would need to make the dresses and suits: thread, beads, and needles, along with a workspace big enough for them to spread open the fabric so they could see what they were making. They would have to clear out part of the living room, she resolved. When Kamila had visited Karteh Parwan, Malika had generously offered to lend one of her trusted "zigzags"; now the younger sister was tempted to accept the offer. If they delivered their work on time and were able to win more orders, maybe they would even be able to buy another machine for all of them to share. Who knows, perhaps one day they would have work for some other girls in their neighborhood who were stuck at home just as they were. All of this, however, was still a long way off. Right now, beginning this very evening, there was a great deal of sewing and teaching to attend to.

At last they crossed the barren courtyard and burst into the house. Kamila tossed her empty black bag onto the floor near the door and walked into the living room, where Saaman and Laila waited anxiously. The girls unleashed a barrage of questions as soon as their siblings entered the living room.

Kamila assured them they had made it just fine, and traced their route through the backstreets of Khair Khana. No, they hadn't seen anything bad or had any trouble and yes, they saw the shopkeeper. . . .

She paused for a moment to let the anticipation build.

"I have some news," she started. Both her tone and her face were stony and serious.

"We got an order!"

A triumphant smile spread across her cheeks, and the girls broke out in a ripple of relieved laughter.

"Oh, that is excellent!" cried Laila, applauding her sister's work. She, too, was full of enthusiasm now that they finally had an important task ahead of them. "Well done, Kamila Jan. Now we have to get started! What are we supposed to make?"

Kamila grinned at her sister's impetuousness. She was delighted to see that the girls were as excited as she was, and that they were ready to begin that very minute. At least we have a lot of energy, she thought, even if none of us has any experience!

Kamila described Mehrab's order and told her sisters they would have to learn to sew quickly. "It won't be easy," she assured them, "but I am sure we can get it done. If I can learn, so can you!"

"We will be fine, Kamila," said Saaman, confident and poised as always. "If we have to ask our friends for help, we will."

"Okay, then," Kamila answered, "we'll get started with our first sewing lesson after lunch. We are officially in business!"

"And you must call her Roya now," Rahim advised his sisters. The girls looked at Kamila, eager for an explanation.

Kamila recounted the story, explaining how her false identity would protect both her and Mehrab the shopkeeper. He wouldn't be able to identify her should the Taliban ever question him for speaking to or, much worse, doing business with a woman at the bazaar. No one at Lycée Myriam would ever see Kamila's face under the chadri, and none of their neighbors had ever heard of Roya. She was safe, at least for now, and she urged her sisters to remember to call her Roya if they ever accompanied her to the market. Kamila/Roya felt relieved to see that her sisters understood the need for her alias. And she appreciated the look of respect they showed her for her quick—and smart—thinking on the spot.

Malika would be proud, Kamila thought, smiling inwardly.

The idea of getting to work thrilled Saaman and Laila, though they had no idea how they would learn to sew in time to deliver according to their sister's schedule. Like Kamila, Saaman had always been absorbed in her studies and had never before made anything by hand. She confided to her sister that she was nervous she would make hundreds of mistakes and ruin their first order. Laila showed far less hesitation; the bold teenager figured the only way she was going to become a good dressmaker was by trying. Just as Malika had shown her in her corner workspace in Karteh Parwan, Kamila began by teaching her sisters how to cut the fabric. Laila followed along, making only a few small mistakes as she went. Saaman, the most studious among them, watched motionless, and fixed her gaze on Kamila's steady hand as it cut the material.

"Come on," Laila ribbed Saaman, "it's not so hard, just try it!"

Elated as she was about receiving her first order, Kamila too felt nervous. Right now she was the only one who knew anything about sewing—and she hardly qualified as an experienced tailor. She had to get this right if they were to attract more business.

And then, quite unexpectedly, as if in answer to her prayers, came the best news she could have asked for.

"Kamila, Kamila, did you hear?" cried Rahim, running into the living room to find his sister. She sat sewing on the floor, lost in her work trying to pin an unruly bead onto a piece of fabric.

"Malika is coming home. She'll be here tomorrow!"

"What?" said Kamila. "Tomorrow? Oh, that is just wonderful!"

She put down her sewing and basked in relief. Malika had always been the dependable big sister, the reliable one who had kept her younger siblings out of trouble. Right now they needed her steady hand. Kamila herself was only a teenager, and she was finding it hard to focus on her business while keeping an eye on her four younger sisters, helping Rahim with his classwork, and making sure they had enough food and fuel to keep the house functioning.

"Yes," said Rahim, "Najeeb talked to her about it before he went. He thought it would be better if we all lived together. It took a little while for her and Farzan to arrange everything, especially with the twins, but his family agreed it would be better if they came here."

The twins. Kamila was as delighted to spend more time with her newborn nieces as she was to see her sister. And she was thrilled at the prospect of being able to return the favor and help Malika, who had given birth to the babies prematurely just two months earlier. She got up from her seat and walked into Malika's old room to begin sweeping out her younger sisters' things.

Every time I think things are bad, something happens, and we get through it, Kamila thought to herself. Father was right; we just have to keep doing our part and everything will be okay. God is watching out for us.

Days later the girls filled with joy at the sight of one of Kabul's familiar yellow-and-white taxis pulling up to their green gate. Malika was back.

❋

Since the arrival of the Taliban several months earlier, life had quickly devolved into a series of challenges for the twenty-four-year-old mother of four. Her sisters may have seen her as their rock, but Malika and her husband, Farzan, were reeling both financially and emotionally. With women barred from schools she could no longer work, so her family had to survive without her monthly teacher's salary. Now, with the economy shrinking by the day and fewer and fewer goods coming in and out of Kabul, demand for Farzan's trucking business had dried up to almost zero. In just months the family had gone from two incomes to less than one.

Malika's tailoring work plus a small amount of savings kept the family going. But she worried constantly about her children. Her twin girls had been born weeks early and had been fighting off infections ever since. In a city which so many doctors had fled and where the infrastructure and sanitation systems had been wrecked by decades of war, this was nearly a death sentence. The babies remained tiny and frail, and Malika shuttled them regularly to the clinic, struggling to fill their expensive prescriptions. Now back in Khair Khana she saw how fragile things were in her parents' home, and how much her sisters—and everyone else in her life—needed her. She was exhausted, but determined to do all that the moment demanded: to be a mentor for her sisters' new tailoring operation, and to continue her own work sewing suits and dresses for clients who valued her skill and creativity. Above all else, she would care for her struggling family. Though it had been hard to leave her friends and in-laws in Karteh Parwan, she knew her place was here in Khair Khana with her sisters.

By the time Malika arrived, the girls had managed to finish most of their first order. The days had rolled by quickly, and soon after they began their new commission they invited Razia, a neighbor and friend, to join them. Kamila had told her about the tailoring work, and Razia had been eager to join so she could help her own family. Her father was too old to work, and her older brother, like Kamila's, had been forced to leave Kabul because of security issues. With no money coming in each month her parents could barely cover even the basics of food and winter clothing. For their part, the girls were happy to have another pair of hands and the company of an old friend they could trust. As she sat with her friends on pillows in the living room sewing the last of the dresses, cups of now-cold chai sitting in front of them, Razia watched the hours speed by. She felt lucky to be able to think about something other than her family's troubles. She told Kamila how happy she was to be working, and the two of them began exchanging ideas for expansion.

"I think there are other tailors who would be interested in our work," Kamila said. "We just need to find them."

Razia was ready to assist Kamila with anything the business needed, including finding more women to help. "I could ask around the neighborhood," she volunteered, "but only to friends we can trust, of course." With stories circulating of neighbors informing on one another to the Amr bil-Maroof, they had to be careful not to work with anyone who would talk about what they were doing. Kamila knew that her team of seamstresses was doing nothing unlawful according to the official rules, which clearly stated that women could work at home so long as they stayed inside and did not mix with men. But no one was safe from the Taliban government's most zealous enforcers. Anything that involved the behavior of women was open to interpretation—and punishment—by the young soldiers on the hunt for offenders day and night. Even behind closed doors the girls had to be cautious.

Despite all the risk, Kamila remained invigorated by

her work, and she began to plan her next trip to Lycée Myriam. The girls had shown her this past week that they were up to the challenge of filling more and even bigger orders. Almost without trying they had settled into a routine that she felt certain would allow them to grow their fledgling venture. In the mornings they would rise at around six-thirty or seven, washing and saying their prayers before moving on to breakfast and finishing their pieces from the evening before. Late in the morning they began reviewing the items they had finished the day before and cutting fabric for the next set of dresses and suits.

Kamila acted as the team's quality control officer, checking everyone's handiwork to make certain that each stitch lived up to the standard Malika had set. Saaman continued to be cautious about cutting without Kamila's supervision, and Kamila continued to remind her that she really didn't need help—she was learning fast and was becoming an excellent tailor, even better than Kamila herself. At noon they would stop for prayers and lunch before returning to their needles. After prayers and dinner, they would heat the wood-fired *bukhari* and sit together by the orange glow of the hurricane lamps, sewing until late in the night. Most of the time the girls worked in silence, engrossed in their fabric and fully focused on their deadline.

The high walls of their courtyard prevented anyone in the street from seeing inside, so Kamila had little fear about curious or nosy passersby asking unwanted questions. And with Malika in the house she had someone to turn to for help if things went wrong. She prayed they never would.

❋

Soon after Malika's arrival, Kamila stopped by her sister's room to see how she was settling in. She found Malika putting her husband's and children's things in a small cupboard.

"How are you?" Kamila asked.

"Oh, we'll be fine," Malika said, deflecting the question. Though she was still a very young woman, she had always worn the air of a wise elder. Kamila thought Malika looked paler and a bit thinner than usual. Still, it was the older girl who reached out, trying to reassure her sister—and also, perhaps, herself—that everything would be all right. "It's so good for the children to be with all of you—I'm glad we're here. How is your work coming?"

"Pretty good, though not as well as if you had done it!" Kamila answered. "I tried to remember everything from our lessons, but it's much harder than I thought, to be honest. I think we have managed okay, though."

She continued: "Maybe you could take a look at some of our dresses?"

Malika welcomed a break from all the unpacking. Within moments Kamila had summoned her younger sisters and they now stood in the small room holding armfuls of new clothing. Malika turned each of the garments inside out and examined the stitches and the seams; then she held each dress up to the girls to judge their proportions, and to see how they hung. Saaman and Laila stood in an expectant silence as Malika studied their work with excruciating attention. After several minutes, she offered her assessment.

"The work is very good," she said, smiling at the girls. A light-colored dress still hung draped over her elbow. "There are a few things I will teach you to make it even better, but overall you've done an excellent job. Kamila has been a very good teacher. But Kamila, you need some help with this belt—we can work on it this afternoon."

The following evening, Kamila readied the dresses and pantsuits—some of them now with particularly handsome belts—for delivery to Mehrab's store. She folded each item with great care, one end over the other, a total of four times to form a neat square, before placing it in a clear plastic bag she then folded and sealed. When she had finished, Kamila slid the garments into two white grocery bags and lined them up carefully near the door.

"I really think this business will work," Kamila told her sister as they sat in the living room sipping tea. Three of Malika's children had gone to sleep a few hours earlier, and she was finally enjoying a moment of quiet before falling into her own bed after the long day. "The girls are doing very well. And it's so good for us to think about work and business instead of just sitting around here all day feeling bored and anxious. Now I just have to find more orders at Lycée Myriam tomorrow. We need more work!"

"Kamila Jan, I'm nervous about you going to the market," Malika replied. One of the twins was running a fever and now slept uneasily against her shoulder. "The more work you get, the more you will have to be there and the more likely it is that something could go wrong."

Kamila could not disagree. But now that she had begun to see the possibilities, she had no intention of stopping. Their work could do a great deal of good for their own family—and maybe even some others in the neighborhood. Now, perhaps more than ever before, they must push forward.

"I know," she said. And she left it at that.

❈

At ten o'clock the next morning Kamila set out for Lycée Myriam with Rahim, who had gone to school in his new white turban only long enough to see that there were not enough teachers for all the students who had assembled for class. Women had accounted for well over half of all educators before the Taliban arrived; now that they couldn't work, their male colleagues scrambled to keep up with the demands of educating all the city's boys and implementing the Taliban's new, more religiously focused curriculum. Lacking teachers, a number of schools had shut their doors, but Rahim's Khair Khana classrooms had remained open and were now absorbing students from nearby neighborhoods. Like all the boys in his class, Rahim now had to balance his schoolwork with his *mahram* duties; he knew as well as the girls did that family came first, and his sisters needed him at home.

Heading off with Rahim, Kamila put on her floor-length coat and held the straps of her square black bag close to her. Again they took the back roads, but this time they moved more quickly once they reached the bazaar. They passed several Amr bil-Maroof milling around the market; Kamila kept her head down and her brother nearby. At last they reached their destination. Kamila checked to make sure that the store was empty and that there were no Taliban in the hall outside, then she followed her brother into Mehrab's shop. With a sigh of relief only she could hear, she placed the meticulously packed stack of handmade dresses and suits on the counter.

"Hello, I am Roya," she said. "This is my brother, and we are here to deliver your order as we discussed last week."

Mehrab looked nervously past Kamila to check for himself that no one was watching, then quickly counted the pile of clothing in front of him. He took one dress and one pantsuit from the plastic bags to inspect the quality of the work.

"These will do," he said after spending a moment looking at the garments. "They are good, but if you made this seam smaller on the pants and added some more beading to the belt on the dress, they would be even better."

"Thank you," she said. "We'll make sure to make those changes for the next order." That presumed, of course, that there would be a next order, she thought to herself.

Mehrab opened a drawer beneath the counter and handed Kamila an envelope filled with afghani, enough to buy the family flour and groceries for a week. Kamila's heart soared. At last she could see real, tangible progress for all the work they had done and the risks she had taken. She wanted to jump up and down with excitement and count the money right then and there. But instead she calmly took the pile of blue-, rose-, and green-colored notes and placed it at the bottom of her bag.

"Would you like to order anything else?" she asked, trying not to sound too eager. "My brother and I can come back next week if there is anything you need."

Mehrab said he would take three more pantsuits in the traditional style. He would wait on the dresses until he saw how the first ones sold. Kamila thanked him for his business. Afterward, she rushed back out to the street, intent on getting them out of Lycée Myriam well before the call to prayer, as she had promised her sisters she would.

Before she had taken even one hundred steps, however, a small side street caught Kamila's attention. Straight ahead and to the left, just off the stony and well-trodden path leading from the road, she saw a red and white walkway.

"Rahim, do you think that is the street with the shop that Zalbi mentioned?"

"I don't know, Roya," he said, smiling at his sister's tenacity, "but I am sure we are about to find out!"

Nearly all the boys in school had sisters working at home, and Rahim's classmate Zalbi had recently told him about a family friend who ran a tailoring shop nearby. "He is a very good man; maybe he would want to buy your dresses," Zalbi had said. It was important to work with honorable people they could trust, and Kamila had been eager to meet the shopkeeper. Now was as good a time as any, she thought, feeling hopeful. Besides, if this was the street, it wouldn't be nearly so easy to spot from the main road, and that would make orders and deliveries a bit easier. Peering out to the left and right to make sure no one was paying them any attention, Kamila headed down the walkway with her brother in search of a new customer.

# 5

# An Idea Is Born . . . but Will It Work?

urning down the wide alleyway, Kamila and Rahim left the bustle of the bazaar behind them. Kamila slowed her steps and allowed herself just a moment to enjoy the stillness of the lane after the tense half hour she had spent trying to make them both invisible in the heart of the Lycée Myriam bazaar. She was grateful for the silence of the barren side street.

As she walked, Kamila scanned the storefronts on each side of the road, spotting stores that sold fabric, kitchen supplies, and shoes. Almost none of them had any customers. Nearing the end of the narrow open-air strip mall, they at last came upon a modest tailoring shop with long, narrow windows that faced the street. Women's dresses hung neatly next to one another in a pastel rainbow that lined the walls inside. The name "Sadaf" was hand-painted on a weather-beaten sign that had been nailed to a cement overhang above the doorway.

"I think this is it," said Rahim.

Kamila nodded.

"Let me do the talking," she said. "If he doesn't seem like someone we can trust, we'll just walk right back out, okay?"

Kamila was nervous as they entered the small, threadbare shop. She struggled to make out the details of the store through the late morning shadows that hung over the white walls and bare floor. Like most of Kabul's businesses, Sadaf had no electricity and relied instead on the sunlight that crept in during the daytime hours.

Fighting back her fear, Kamila momentarily paused at the entrance, holding the doorknob tight, but she quickly reminded herself of everyone back home who was counting on her.

I can't be scared, she thought. I'm doing this for my family, and Allah will help to keep us safe.

As the door slammed closed behind her, the shopkeeper looked up from the counter. He was folding long dresses and roomy, wide-legged pants like the ones Kamila had seen through the window. His clothes were among the prettiest samples she had seen of Taliban-era fashion.

Sadaf's inventory clearly matched the times. The shop-keeper was young, maybe Kamila's own age, with a bushy beard that overwhelmed his narrow chin. His bright eyes looked remarkably kind.

"Good morning," he said. "May I help you, sister? Can I show you anything?"

He was extremely polite—much more so than Mehrab. Kamila felt her confidence returning.

"No, thank you, sir," Kamila began. "My name is Roya; my sisters and I are tailors in Khair Khana. My brother here is helping us. His friend Zalbi is a friend of your family's and he suggested we come to see you. We're looking for work and we would be very glad to make some dresses for your store if you are interested."

"I am Ali," he replied, clasping Rahim's hand. "It's a pleasure to meet you. I would be glad to see your work if you've brought any with you. My brother and I are looking for seamstresses to make dresses for us."

Judging by the fact that he had set up shop in Khair Khana, a largely Tajik suburb that was home to many families from Parwan and Panjshir, plus the lilt of his Shomali accent, Kamila guessed that Ali's parents, like hers, were from the north. That they were conversing in Dari, the Persian language spoken in the northern regions, rather than Pashto, the traditional language of the Pashtun south, made her more certain of it.

"I hope your family is doing well," said Kamila. "My

brother and sisters and I are working to support ourselves while our parents are in the north. My father is in Parwan and our older brother had to go to Pakistan because of security. We've started a dressmaking business in our house and we'd really appreciate your support."

The young man returned Kamila's good wishes for her family and added that his parents too were from Parwan. The three teenagers shared the news and the rumors they'd heard about the recent fighting in the north. Then Ali began to tell Kamila a bit of his own story.

"Sadaf is my store," he said. "I've put nearly everything I have into it. Before the Taliban I had a pushcart selling linens and kitchen supplies. But then everyone stopped buying. And it got too dangerous to be out on the street all day. So I started my shop here. At least I know that people will always need clothing, even if they're buying less of it now."

Ali looked down as if he were going to stop speaking. Kamila realized with some surprise that she and the shopkeeper had a lot in common. They were both young people caught in circumstances they had had nothing to do with, who were fighting as hard as they could to take care of their very large families. Right now, Ali had more than a dozen relatives depending upon him for food and shelter.

"One of my brothers, Mahmood, just fled Jabul Saraj," Ali continued, referring to the mountain-ringed town just south of Kamila's parents in Parwan. Kamila knew from the radio and neighbors' reports that the town was now a major battleground in the war between the Taliban and Massoud.

"He had been working in our family's grocery shop since he finished his army service a few years ago. When the front line of the war moved to Jabul Saraj, he took his wife and little children to the Salang mountain pass to wait out the fighting. They walked for three hours to reach the mountains and slept outside that night with many other families. The next day people tried to tell him it was safe to go home, but my brother knew better—the fighting had just started, it wasn't even close to ending. So he fled with his family through Khinjan and Poli Khumri to Mazar. They stayed there with some of our relatives for a few months, but finding work was very hard, and Mahmood has a big family to support. Finally he decided to come here to try to earn a living. There's only one way into Kabul now because of all the fighting, you know, and the trip from Mazar took him three full days. Anyway, I helped him open his own tailoring shop just down the street. He was worried at first because he didn't know anything about women's clothing, but I told him that he knew plenty about sales from running our parents' store and that that was much more important. We can rely on seamstresses from the neighborhood for our merchandise."

When Ali finished his story, Kamila assured him that

she and her sisters would be happy to help Mahmood fill his store with inventory whenever he needed it.

"Well then, let's see what kind of work you are doing," he said.

Kamila swiftly unfolded her sample and spread it out on the display case. Ali inspected the dress closely, flipping it front and back and examining the hand-stitched hems. "It's very nice work," he said. "I'll take six dresses and, if you can make them, four pantsuits.

"But see here," he continued, still studying the garment. "Can you change this detail along the waist of the dress?" Kamila quickly agreed, and committed the details of the waistline to memory—she didn't want to waste time and, besides, drawing was illegal now. Ali then walked around the counter and moved toward the front window looking out over the street. He pointed to a lovely white wedding dress that was hanging there.

"Roya, do you think you and your sisters could make these?" he asked. "They're a bit more complicated and will probably take a little longer, but that is no problem."

Kamila didn't have to think about it; she immediately said, "Of course." Laila's impetuousness had become infectious, she realized, smiling. Ali took one of the long-sleeved beaded bridal gowns down from its display and handed it to Kamila to use as a model. "I'll take three of these, and we can see how it goes from there."

Kamila thanked Ali for his business.

"This means a lot to my family," she said. "We won't let you down."

"Thank you, sister," said Ali. "May God keep you and your family safe."

With that, Kamila and Rahim left the store for the street and headed home once more. By now they were perilously close to the noontime call to prayer, but Kamila was thrilled about having a new customer for her slowly expanding business. This is how it starts, Kamila thought. Now we just have to keep it growing. And we have to make sure nothing goes wrong.

Walking home, Kamila thought about whether they would need help, in the form of more seamstresses, to complete the orders for Mehrab and Ali. Right now they were getting by, but that was hardly enough; with the new orders coming in, they needed a better, more streamlined process. Most of all, they needed more hands. She would speak with her sisters about it tonight. In the meantime, she had the wedding dresses to think about.

After dinner the sisters settled into the living room to begin the evening's sewing. Kamila lit the hurricane lamps so they could see what they were doing. Just for a second she indulged a thought about how much easier electricity would have made their work. What a luxury it would be to flip a switch and have the room light up and the sewing machines begin humming!

"So I think we need to make a few changes," Kamila

said to the girls. "We have more orders now, and we need help. Do you guys have any ideas?"

Saaman, Laila, and even their youngest sister, Nasrin, chimed in at once, each trying to speak over the other. Yes, they surely did have ideas!

"Okay, okay," Kamila said, laughing at the cacophony of voices that filled their makeshift workspace. "One at a time!"

"What if we divide up the cutting and beading—make it something like an assembly line, so that one person is responsible for each," Saaman said. "Whoever is best at cutting can do it for all of us. That would help the dresses look a little more professional, too."

Nasrin nodded. "I agree. I also think we should clear out this room to make more space to sew. Mother isn't here in her usual place, and Father doesn't need his seat in front of the radio anymore. We might as well turn this into a real workshop. When they return, we can put things back just as they were. Also, I think Malika would like to have a bigger place to work, and Rahim won't mind. So really, there's nothing to stop us from using the space however we like."

"Nasrin, you are going to have us turn the entire house into a little factory!" Kamila said, breaking out into a giggle. "Our own parents wouldn't recognize their own home!"

Laila chimed in to support her little sister.

"Nasrin is right. It's a pain to have to put away our work every evening. It would be much easier if we could keep everything out. I think it will save us some time, too!"

A sense of purpose drove the discussion, and Kamila saw clearly that the business had become the main focus of their days. Together they had found a way to be productive in spite of their confinement. And with so much work in front of them, they almost forgot about all the problems of the world outside.

"There's one other thing I want to mention, since we're talking about the business," Kamila told her sisters. "Both Mehrab and Ali said other women had come to them with dresses to sell. We really need to make sure our work is as creative, beautiful, and professional as possible. And if we commit to a deadline, we have to deliver on time, no matter how large the order is. We want them to know us as reliable girls who make the dresses that their customers want to buy. Razia is coming over later; let's ask her for ideas about other girls in Khair Khana who might be able to come over and sew with us. And we'll definitely need some help from Malika on those wedding dresses."

Since her return to Khair Khana, Malika's business had also begun to prosper—at least by the standards of the current economy, in which mere survival constituted success. It had begun with women who came to see her from her old neighborhood of Karteh Parwan. Then women in

Khair Khana began to hear from friends and neighbors that there was a master tailor living among them who could meet some of their fancier clothing needs. Most of Malika's clients were slightly older women who had lived through so many of Kabul's changes these past thirty years, from the relative freedom of the 1970s and 1980s through the stricter Mujahideen dress code of the last five years and now this, the time of the chadri. They knew they must stay within the limits of what was permitted by the Taliban but refused to completely shed their own sense of style. It was a delicate balance that Malika had instinctively understood and come to master.

By now, a few new customers were stopping by each week to place orders for her elegant dresses and pantsuits. Malika's designs retained the distinctly Afghan broad sleeves and legs and baggy fit, but also reflected her appreciation for the French-style cuts that had been so popular in Kabul in the 1970s and 1980s. Before the Taliban, Malika had occasionally shopped the used clothing stalls at her bazaar in Karteh Parwan for the Western-style dresses or skirt suits seen in the capital during the royal family's reform era and, later, the period of Dr. Najibullah's rule. She would take the garments home and disassemble them so she could see and learn how the seams fit together and which fabrics worked best for the different styles she was trying to achieve.

Women ordered Malika's more elaborate party dresses

for wedding celebrations and Eid, the holiday marking the end of the holy month of Ramadan. But with the fighting still going on and the economy in a tailspin, weddings, which had always been ornate and expensive affairs in Afghanistan, seemed to be happening far less often. To begin with, many men had gone to fight on the front lines. And others had left Afghanistan to find work elsewhere, shrinking the pool of potential grooms. Because so many families had fled to Pakistan or Iran, there were fewer aunts, uncles, and cousins to invite. Those who remained in Kabul could hardly afford the days-long celebrations that in good times could easily cost as much as ten thousand dollars—an astronomical sum that forced many grooms into lifelong debt—and sometimes much more than that. Everyone knew that any sort of social gathering could bring trouble, and stories spread of Taliban soldiers bursting into people's living rooms to break up wedding parties on suspicion that guests might be dancing or playing music, including the *dhol*, the Afghan two-sided drum, in violation of the new rules. The worst of these incidents ended with the Taliban hauling male guests—and sometimes even the groom—off to prison, where they would remain for a few days until family members could either plead or pay their way out.

All of this meant that those weddings that did occur were somber and far shorter events with a ceremony at home followed by a simple dinner of chicken and pilau.

So Malika adapted her style to suit the times. None of her dresses were too fitted or too Western; arms and necks were fully covered and gowns reached well past the floor so no shoes would ever show. Women did, of course, still want to be beautiful for their wedding day, so Malika ensured that the beading and the embroidery were elaborate enough for her brides to feel supremely regal while remaining within the government-mandated sartorial boundaries.

With each week, Malika's queue of orders grew longer. Customers now waited for as long as two weeks for their garments. This rising demand compelled the working mother to stretch her days even longer, for she, like Kamila, was determined to make sure her clients kept coming back. She rose earlier each morning and, after washing and saying her prayers, rushed to get her oldest son, Saeed, ready for school before making sure that four-year-old Hossein was fed and ready for the day. Then she would carry the twins' wooden crib out into the living room and set it up next to her workspace. The infants slept most of the morning as she sewed, and she left her work only to tend to them when they awoke hungry or in need of a new diaper. Throughout the day Kamila and the other girls would take a break from their own dressmaking to visit their little nieces. They carried them around the living room and sang lullabies and old Afghan ballads until the babies were ready to eat and return to sleep once more. Then everyone went back to work.

At Kamila's request Malika led an improvised version of a sewing "master class" for the girls. First she walked them through the basics of making a wedding dress, and then showed them the difference between Mehrab's dress and Ali's. Next came the pantsuits.

"Be creative," Malika urged the girls. "This is how your dresses will stand out from the others that are in the stores. Don't be afraid to try new ideas; if they don't work, they won't sell!"

The young women learned quickly, picking up new sewing techniques before the afternoon was over. Watching the girls hone their skills, and seeing the enthusiasm with which they embraced Malika's teaching and advice, Kamila felt increasingly certain of their little venture's business potential.

As the afternoon sank into evening, they heard a knock at the door. Kamila thought it must be Razia, but she usually let herself in. The girls said nothing to each other, but their forced calm spoke volumes: surprises were unwelcome and fear was now the normal reaction to any unexpected visitor.

Kamila called to Rahim to open the gate. After just a moment, she saw with relief her aunt Huma hurrying through the doorway with her fifteen-year-old daughter, Farah, at her side. Once inside, the women pulled back their chadri. A waterfall of blue fabric cascaded down their backs and onto the floor.

Laila was the first to the door, and she threw her arms around her aunt. Huma in turn kissed each of the girls, one by one. It was the closest to a maternal embrace they had had in ages.

"I'm so glad to see you; we've been thinking about you but didn't know whether you were still here in Kabul," Kamila said. "Come sit and have something to eat."

After asking about their parents and making sure the girls were doing well, Huma came to the point of her visit. No calls were purely social anymore.

"Is Malika Jan here?" she asked.

The older girl had left her work for just a moment to check on Saeed, and when she returned she greeted her aunt with a warm embrace.

"Hello, Auntie. Is everything okay?"

"Well, that's why we've come, Malika Jan," Huma replied. "We are all healthy and well, but the situation here is getting very dangerous, as you know. We can't stay in Kabul any longer. I've decided to take the girls to Pakistan. We leave tomorrow." She paused for a moment. "We want you to come with us."

All the Sidiqi sisters stood huddled around their aunt, holding their collective breath. They knew where this conversation was headed. It was the same discussion they had had with their parents months earlier, when Mr. Sidiqi had decided that it was safer for the girls to remain in Kabul rather than risk the journey to Pakistan or Iran.

"Of course if your sisters are permitted to come, we want them to join us, but I know your father thinks it safest for them to remain here together," the older woman said. "I would not challenge his wishes, of course."

"Thank you, Auntie. You know we appreciate your thinking of us and that we're very grateful for your kindness," said Malika. All the while she was staring at Huma's hands; it was obvious to everyone that she didn't dare to meet her aunt's eyes, lest she unleash tears from her own. "I will talk with Farzan, but honestly I don't think he will change his mind. We are planning to stay here; it's just too difficult and expensive to travel with so many small children, and I can't think about leaving the girls behind." She nodded toward her sisters. "Allah will protect us; please don't worry."

Huma had come prepared for this argument, and she began to list all the reasons why Malika's family and the Sidiqi girls should leave with them: First, no one was left in the city and the capital's problems would only get worse. There were no jobs for any of them and there was no reason she could think of to believe this would change anytime soon. It was simply not safe to stay, she insisted. "There is no future here for you girls." Finally, Huma added that she and her daughters would be safer if Malika's family joined them on the journey to Pakistan. "It's better for everyone if we leave together, as a family, and there's no time to waste."

Malika again promised that she would speak with her husband, but her quiet voice now betrayed months of worry and exhaustion. All the girls felt for their aunt, a middle-aged woman who had been left on her own in the city with two teenage daughters to care for, but they had no choice but to turn down her plea for help.

With nothing more to be said and nightfall approaching, the women once again exchanged hugs and kisses, this time in sadness rather than joy. Malika embraced her aunt a moment longer than usual.

"I will be thinking of all of you," she said, "and I know God will protect you and your girls." Later that night, alone with her thoughts, Kamila lay in bed replaying the evening's events. "We will be on our own here for a while," she told herself, "and we had better find a way to make the best of it, just as we always have." She resolved to stay focused on her siblings and her business instead of dwelling on all that she couldn't change, like the separation of her family, the education she was missing out on, and the fate of her cousins who were about to embark on the perilous journey to Pakistan.

The weeks passed in a blur of beaded dresses and pantsuits. Days started with prayers and breakfast and ended fourteen hours later with the girls falling into bed, exhausted but already planning for the next morning's sewing. Kamila, meanwhile, was getting better at winning new business, with the help of her *mahram* Rahim.

Of all of her siblings, Rahim had become the one Kamila now relied on the most. He was her faithful guard and gofer, and a trusted colleague in her small business. He may have been a teenager, but he never complained when his sisters asked him to go out for whatever sewing supplies they needed, or to run to the market for rice or sugar. She had no idea how they would have gotten by without his energy and kindness.

Kamila and Rahim went out more and more often these days. Refusing her sisters' pleas to be satisfied with the marginal victories of slightly larger orders, Kamila pressed ahead with expanding their customer base and growing their venture. Following Ali's introduction, she was now taking orders for Ali's brother, Mahmood. That brought their customers to three. Kamila told the girls that she and Rahim would try to find introductions to more tailors they knew they could trust, once she was certain they could successfully juggle all the work they had now.

❋

After breakfast one morning Kamila heard the gate rattle. She had been up since six-thirty finishing the beading on a dress for Ali. The girls looked around to see whether anyone was expecting a visitor before asking Rahim to see who was there. They waited anxiously until their brother returned to the sitting room with a tall woman with long brown hair and one of the saddest but most serene faces

Kamila had ever seen. Kamila guessed she was around thirty years old.

"Kamila Jan," said Rahim, "our guest is here to see you."

Kamila held out her hand and kissed the stranger in the traditional Afghan show of respect, three times on alternating cheeks.

"Hello, I am Kamila," she said. "How are you? May I help you with something?"

The woman was pale and looked exhausted. Light brown circles hung beneath her eyes.

"My name is Sara," she said. "I've come here hoping you might have some work." She stared down at her feet while her words came out in a slow and melancholy succession. "My cousin's neighbor told me that you are running a tailoring business here with your sisters, and that you are a very kind woman. She said that your business is doing well and that perhaps you could use some help."

Just then Laila arrived and handed a glass of steaming tea to the visitor. She moved a small silver bowl filled with bright taffy candies in front of their guest.

"Please, sit down," Kamila urged, pointing toward the floor.

Sara lowered herself onto a pillow. Gripping her glass tightly, she began to explain how she had ended up in Kamila's sitting room.

"My husband died two years ago," she said, her gaze focused on the tasseled corner of the carpet. "He was the director of the high school Lycée Ariana. One afternoon he came home from school saying he didn't feel well. He went to the doctor that afternoon to see what was wrong, and he was gone a day later."

Kamila nodded, warmly urging her guest to continue.

"Since then, my three children and I have been living with my husband's brothers here in Khair Khana. My daughter is five, and she is disabled. My sons are seven and nine. My husband's family is very kind, but there are fifteen of us at home to support, and now my brothers-in-law are facing their own problems."

One, she told Kamila, had worked as an airplane mechanic for the army. He was now out of work since Massoud's forces had fled northward. Another had been a city official, and he too had been laid off. A third brother-in-law was a computer scientist, but he couldn't find a job in Kabul and was thinking about leaving for Pakistan or Iran.

"I have to find a way to support my children," Sara told Kamila. "I don't know what else to do, or where else to go. My husband's family can't care for us much longer, and I don't want to be a burden to them all. I must find a job."

Pausing only long enough to take a sip of tea and to make certain that Kamila was still listening, she went on: "I am not an educated woman, and I've never had a job before. But I know how to sew, and I will do a good job for you. I promise."

At first Kamila was too moved to speak. Everyone who had remained in Kabul had a similar story, and lately she had been feeling a growing sense of responsibility to do as much as she possibly could to help. Her father had told her, and her religion had taught her, that she had a duty to support as many as she was able. Right now that meant she must quickly build upon the modest successes they had achieved so far. This business was her best—and right now her only—hope for helping her community.

"Let's get to work, then," Kamila said, regaining her composure and finding comfort in her own practical approach. "What we need most right now is a supervisor who can watch over everything and help me make sure all the orders are filled and the sewing is done well." Sara, now smiling for the first time since she walked through the door, would be their first official employee.

She reported for her first day of work promptly at eight-thirty the next morning. Her three children stayed at home with her sisters-in-law. Like Rahim, her two boys were in school part of the day in Khair Khana. Her father-in-law was helping them to learn the parts of their studies that were now conducted in Arabic—a new part of the Taliban curriculum.

As the division of labor between the two women naturally fell into place, Kamila realized that it had been a brilliant—if rash—decision to hire Sara. Her new supervisor was a talented seamstress who was able to help the girls with more complicated designs, sparing Malika the interruptions that had become so common. But she was also a good manager—in fact she was a natural. She knew when to push the girls and when to encourage them, and she held the entire team to the highest standard: if a seam was off or a beaded design strayed too far outside the lines of their stencil designs, she would push a girl to start again, sometimes taking the stitches out and resewing them herself.

Even more important, Sara's contribution freed Kamila to focus on the part of the operation she was coming to love most, despite all the risks: the marketing and the planning. Each week Kamila was growing more sure of herself and her sisters' sewing skills, and more comfortable moving with Rahim around Lycée Myriam, whose sounds and smells and shadows she was coming to know as intimately as her own neighborhood's. The group had gained experience and grown its team of seamstresses, and the girls were learning to handle the bigger jobs that clients were offering now that they had proven themselves to be reliable and professional. Only a few weeks after Sara arrived, Kamila was thrilled to accept an order for twenty lightweight dresses from Ali, who wanted to stock up for spring.

To make certain that they brought on only the most

committed candidates with the strongest work ethic, Kamila and Razia developed a new interviewing process. They gave aspiring seamstresses a swath of fabric and asked for a sample of their work. Sara would then review the finished piece, and if the sewing passed muster, the new girl would receive her first assignment, which she could make either at her own home or at Kamila's house. All orders would be due within a week.

It wasn't long before the demand for work outpaced the orders Kamila was receiving from shopkeepers. She now received visits almost daily from young women who were trying to help out their families. Most of them were girls whose high school and university studies had been cut short by the Taliban's arrival, but some of them, like Sara, were a bit older.

She didn't know how she was going to find a place for all of them, but she was determined to. With the city's economy shrinking and almost no other chances for women to earn money, how could she turn them away?

In the morning she would return to Lycée Myriam with Rahim. She would talk with Ali and Mahmood and ask them to introduce her to a third brother of theirs who had just arrived in Kabul and opened another tailoring shop nearby. She hoped that he too would become a regular customer.

As she approached Malika's room to wish her a good night, an idea occurred to Kamila. We are seamstresses, yes, but we are also teachers. Isn't there a way we could use both talents to help even more women? And then those women could help us grow our tailoring business so that there would be more work for everyone.

We should start a school, she thought to herself as she stood in the hallway, or at least a more formal apprenticeship for young women, who would learn to sew and embroider with us. We'll teach them valuable skills that they can use here or with other women, and while we're teaching them, we'll be building an in-house team that can help us fill large orders quickly—as many as we can secure.

She stopped in front of Malika's door, lost in her dream. Most of all, she thought, we won't have to turn anyone away. Even the young ones who have no experience and aren't qualified to work yet can join our training program and work for a salary helping us with our orders as soon as they are able. If we have our own school, then no one who comes to our gate will leave without a job.

She had discovered her plan.

Too impatient to knock, Kamila strode into Malika's room nearly bursting with excitement. For the moment she would simply ignore all the obstacles that could prevent her project from becoming reality. She wanted her sister's support and couldn't wait to tell her about the idea. There was no one whose talents and temperament were better suited to such a teaching venture and no one of whose trust she could be more certain. She folded herself up on a pillow next to Malika, who was sorting the day's wash for her husband and four children. With the hurricane lamplight filling the space between them, Kamila eagerly began.

"Malika," she said, looking directly at her sister, "I need your help. . . ."

# 6

# Class Is in Session

Rahim, let's go!" Kamila called to her brother. She looked at the living room clock and saw that it was nearly 9 A.M. They needed to get out the door now. They had deliveries to make at Lycée Myriam, and besides that, Kamila was eager to talk with her brother alone.

The boy put down his half-eaten piece of naan and tea, grabbed his jacket from the hook near the door, and caught up with his sister. She was already in the courtyard.

Kamila had been up most of the evening after her talk with Malika thinking about her plans for the school: the classes they would offer and the pool of talented seamstresses they would create. Once she and the girls had the program running smoothly they would be able to take on new customers. They needed more orders, that was clear; there had to be enough work for all the girls they were training as well as the others who were sewing in their own homes for the Sidiqi sisters.

Kamila wanted to use this morning's outing to hear Rahim's thoughts about the tailoring school. She had faith in his judgment and trusted him to serve as her sounding board; often the two would hatch plans for the sewing business during their long walks to the bazaar, which he now knew nearly as well as Kamila did. He had met all the shopkeepers with his sister "Roya" and earned their trust with his unassuming manner and his unfailing reliability. If Kamila was busy at home finishing up an order or managing the next round of garment making, Rahim would make deliveries in her place, passing along messages from her customers and picking up the next batch of sewing materials on his way home.

Negotiating, however, he left strictly to his sister. The siblings had just taken a battered station wagon taxi all the way downtown to Mandawi Bazaar, the historic market in the old city, where Ali had suggested they could find sewing supplies for much less. Kamila had marched confidently through the bazaar's narrow stalls searching for fabric she liked and haggling with shopkeepers about their prices, which Rahim knew were well below what they usually paid at Lycée Myriam. "Rahim, I think shopping here could lower our costs by ten or maybe even fifteen percent!" she exclaimed, clearly invigorated by their new discovery. "Roya Jan," he said, waiting for the weary fabric salesmen to realize his sister would never budge from the two lak afghani (four dollars) she had already offered for the bolts of material lined up against the mud walls, "I think if you have your way that number will soon be twenty!"

Working alongside the girls, Rahim had come to know the rhythms of their workweek and the cycles of their incoming orders: which dresses needed to be where and when, and whether filling a shopkeeper's rush order entailed just a few extra hours of work or required an all-night sewing session. A few weeks earlier he had even asked Saaman to teach him the basics of beading and embroidery, enough to assist his sisters in making the batches of dresses and pantsuits they were now under contract to produce each week. He would sit with them in the now overcrowded living room during the evenings, the only male in a group of intensely focused women, ready to learn whatever skills he needed to so he could help contribute to the business.

"Rahim, I have a new idea I want to discuss with you," Kamila said.

"A new idea?" he replied. "Why does this not surprise me, Kamila Jan?"

"No, I am very serious," she said, allowing just a little laugh at her own expense. "I want us to start a school. To teach tailoring. This way we can support all the new orders, grow the business, and also support a lot more women in the neighborhood."

She quickened her step. "I've thought the whole thing through and I think this is how we should organize it: We'll have two shifts of girls each day, one in the morning and one in the afternoon, with a break for prayer and lunch in between. Saaman and Laila will teach the students sewing, beading, and embroidery; I will help at first, of course, but I really want the two of them to lead the classes—then I'll be able to focus more on finding new customers for us. Sara Jan will supervise. I spoke with Malika about it last night—she's the only one I've discussed it with other than you—and she thinks it's a very good idea."

She waited just a moment.

"So what do you think?"

Kamila couldn't read Rahim's reaction. When they were out in public he always wore an inscrutable expression that he had begun cultivating the very first day they walked to Lycée Myriam: that of a much older man watching over and protecting the women in his family while they faced the dangers that came with being out in public.

But he was nodding his head in agreement.

"Yes, I think it's a very good idea. For me, it won't make much of a difference, since I'll be at school—at least most of the day. But we are stretched so thin right now. You and the others are working almost all the time—at least eleven or twelve hours a day, and then sometimes the all-nighters for everyone when we get hit with a big order. It's a great problem to have, but I've been worried about how we'll keep up with it over time. You're right, we definitely need more help."

They walked on a bit in silence. Kamila knew he had more to say.

"There's one thing about this, though, that makes me worry," Rahim continued. "How are you going to have all these girls coming and going to our house all day without anyone noticing? The Amr bil-Maroof are everywhere and you know they're always on the lookout for people who are bending the rules. Especially women."

Kamila was expecting this; it had been Malika's concern as well.

"Well, I've thought about this, too," she replied. "First of all, a lot of women are working at home now, like Dr. Maryam. The Taliban know she is just treating sick ladies and trying to help the community, so they don't ever come to her clinic. We'll operate the same way: we'll make sure everyone in our section of Khair Khana knows we are only women sewing—we won't tell them about your embroidery at night!—and that we don't ever, ever allow men or strangers to come to the house. We'll send all the girls who come from the neighborhood home well before dark, so no one coming from our house will ever be seen wandering the streets after hours. Or at the time of prayer. And we'll work as discreetly as possible: we'll be quiet, of course, and we'll keep the gate closed at all times. Plus all the girls will be required to wear the full chadri whenever they come to our house. If we're strict about following these rules, and only work with honorable girls from around here, I think we'll be okay."

"That's true," Rahim agreed. "A lot of my friends from school have mothers and sisters who are working at home. Most of them are teaching the Holy Q'uran and math and Dari lessons. They're not really running businesses, as we are. The tailoring school might actually be easier to manage, since you're just teaching women traditional kinds of handiwork they can do in their own houses.

"So," he continued, "when will you begin?"

"Next week," Kamila said.

"Of course!" Rahim said, unable to suppress a quiet chuckle. "You're Kamila: why wait when you can start right away?"

Kamila grinned back at him from behind her chadri.

"You mean Roya Jan."

"Yes, of course! Let me know how I can help you get things started. And be sure to keep leaving me piles of work I can do when I come back from school. I'm actually getting pretty good at it, you know. A bunch of the boys in my class are learning embroidery and sewing, too, but I don't think any of them has as good a teacher as Saaman."

Instinctively, as they approached Lycée Myriam, they both fell silent.

After they entered Ali's store, Kamila unloaded her

bag and waited quietly as the teenager opened the square bundle and counted the garments inside. Kamila was relieved to see he looked pleased.

Ali placed a handful of the dresses and pantsuits on the wooden shelf behind him, and after glancing at the door he turned back to the siblings.

"I have some news about my older brother Hamid," Ali said, and he began another family story, one Mahmood had hinted at during their delivery trip to his shop the week before. "For years he sold women's perfumes and cosmetics and things in Jabul Saraj, but when the fighting got close, everyone stopped shopping. So he started driving a taxi to help his family. One day he picked up a man who worked with Massoud's forces, and he warned my brother that another Taliban offensive was about to begin. Hamid rushed home to get his wife and his children—he had already tried to send them here with other families to escape the fighting, but their driver had gotten lost during the trip and his wife was too scared to travel without him again. Anyway, at last they've all made it safely here to Kabul."

Ali glanced out the window and continued. "Mahmood and I helped Hamid to open a tailoring shop close by; we figured that would be easiest for everyone, since we have a lot of customers, including Talibs who come to buy dresses for their families. And we know reliable seamstresses like you and your sisters, so stocking his store won't be a problem."

He handed Kamila an envelope with payment for the clothes. "Hamid is just back from Pakistan; he went to buy dresses to sell at his store. But I'd like to introduce you to him; he probably will still want to order a few things from you."

Kamila nodded in gratitude, and in moments the three of them were making their way down the block to a cramped storefront with one rectangular window and an entryway three steps above the street. Inside a man was standing on a stack of boxes putting the final touches on a display of dresses that was hanging from the ceiling. He was taller than Ali and clearly several years older. Heart-shaped red plastic containers and portable grooming kits with small metal scissors filled the display case beneath the glass counter. A stack of black flat shoes with dainty bows sat on their pink boxes against the wall.

Exchanging greetings, the brothers briefly embraced in a loose shoulder hug. Then Ali turned to Kamila and Rahim and announced the reason for their unexpected visit. "Hamid, this is Roya and Roya's brother, Rahim. Their parents are from Parwan and they started a tailoring business with their sisters here in Khair Khana to help support their family. Roya and her sisters are among our best seamstresses; they've made a lot of pantsuits and dresses, and some very nice wedding gowns for my store and Mahmood's. If you have work for her, I know you will find her an honorable and trustworthy person."

Hamid was indeed ready to place an order; his trip to Pakistan had been productive, he told them, but difficult with all the checkpoints. "I don't think I'll be going back there anytime soon." He ordered eight dresses like the beautiful beaded ones he had seen hanging in his brother's shop.

"Once I get more settled, and I know my customers' tastes a little better, we can discuss some other designs," Hamid told Kamila. "Right now I've got my hands full just trying to unpack all the boxes I've brought from my old shop in Jabul Saraj." He handed Rahim a plastic bag that held several bundles of light-colored fabric. "To help your sisters get started on my order."

Time was passing and Kamila was eager to be on her way, but Hamid turned to his younger brother.

"Ali, I saw something terrible the other day," he whispered. "I was delivering the dresses I had brought from Pakistan, and I was in a store over there on the next street waiting for the shopkeeper to pay me. There was a woman shopping with her daughter. She was very old, very small, and she could barely see. So she opened her chadri for only a moment to look at the dresses on the display case. Just then the Amr bil-Maroof came running into the store yelling about how women should never show themselves in public, how it was forbidden. The Talib hit her in the face, knocked her onto the ground. I couldn't believe it. She cried out, asking him why he would hit an old woman who could easily be his grandmother. But the soldier just smacked her again. He said she was an indecent woman and called her all sorts of names. It was unbelievable."

The five of them stood in silence until Ali finally said, "Roya, you'd better be going. We've all been talking for too long. . . . It's not safe." His voice drifted off as he finished his sentence.

"Thank you, both," she replied, while Rahim gathered up their bags. "We'll be back next week with your dresses, Hamid." She and her brother left the store, grateful for the cold spring air that greeted them.

"Please be careful," she heard Ali call out as the door closed behind them. "May God protect you."

They walked without speaking for the next half hour.

❋

Within a week, the school began to take shape. The neighborhood grapevine spread the word that young women were gathering for classes at the Sidiqi home, and students started flocking to the house each morning, ready to learn and to work. Though some schools in the neighborhood were charging a small fee, Kamila had decided it was better not to; the girls would pay nothing while they were learning, and in exchange they wouldn't earn a salary until their training period ended. During their apprenticeship they would help make garments that Kamila could take to the market, so their work would contribute to the business almost immediately. How soon a girl completed her training depended on both her skills and her commitment to her work. Only Kamila and Sara would have the final say on that question, with input from their teachers, Saaman and Laila.

Enthusiastically assisting Kamila and her sisters was their new helper Neelab, a young neighborhood girl whose father was a tailor. Neelab's mother had cornered Kamila in the grocery store across the street one afternoon while she and Rahim were buying oil and rice. She had begged Kamila to take the young girl in. "My husband has no work and we can't afford to feed everyone in our house," the woman had told Kamila, her voice thick with despair. "I hear you and your sisters are running a good business. Can you find work for our daughter? I promise she will work hard for you and do whatever you and your sisters need."

Kamila had agreed on the spot, unable to refuse a neighbor's entreaty. She knew the girl to be a lovely child, respectful and well behaved, and she felt for her mother, who was clearly carrying a heavy burden. But there was another benefit to having her around: she could serve as a *mahram* who could go out in the street and see what was happening when Rahim was at class or away from home. Young girls needed no chadri and often functioned as boys, moving freely in public without being bothered so long as they dressed modestly and looked well below the age at which they must be veiled, which now seemed to fall somewhere around twelve or thirteen, though no one knew for certain.

In only a short time Neelab had proven herself to be an able and hardworking apprentice; she arrived early each morning with a bright smile to help Laila prepare the family's breakfast. Then she turned to the household work and anything else that needed doing, including running out to the store nearby for stray items Rahim might have forgotten or accompanying Kamila on short trips to Lycée Myriam. Neelab was grateful to be there, with girls who enjoyed having her around and appreciated her help. Already she was calling Kamila and Malika her "aunties," a term of respect and endearment for an older woman who, though unrelated by blood, was nonetheless family.

For their part, Neelab's aunties understood only too well the risks involved with growing their venture. Malika and Kamila had discussed them many times, and Kamila had kept her promise to stay well within the boundaries of the Taliban's edicts. Before accepting any of the girls to their program, Kamila and her sisters made sure the students knew the school's rules, and each young woman received a lecture from Sara the day she arrived that laid them out.

"The rules are here to be followed," Sara would tell the girls in a firm voice. "No exceptions. If you have come here to work, you are welcome. If you have come here to goof off or eat a nice lunch or just to have fun, this is not the place for you."

Then she would recite the house regulations.

"First, you must wear a chadri and you must keep it on until you are safely inside the house. A large veil is not enough. We know that chadri are expensive, so if you have a problem paying for it, we can help you. As for your clothing, please stick to simple attire—baggy pants, long-sleeved tops, and no white shoes; that is the color of the Taliban flag and they have forbidden it. And no nail polish. The Taliban can see your hands from underneath the chadri and they always watch out for that.

"Second, no talking loudly or laughing in the streets on your way to this house. Our neighbors support our business because we support the community, and we don't want any problems for them or for us. If the Taliban comes here to crack down on our work, that would be bad news for the girls here but also for all of the families around us.

"Third, never, ever talk to men other than your *mahram* on the way here. If you see other girls who are working here doing so you must tell me immediately. Anyone caught speaking to a man of any age will be asked to leave. At once.

"We have these rules to protect Kamila and her sisters as well as yourself and all the other girls in this house and we don't make any exceptions."

Once she had finished, Sara would soften just a bit.

"So please, for everyone's sake, don't do anything that would jeopardize our work. But while you are here we want you to learn and to have fun."

Three weeks on, the school was growing fast, and so was the number of orders that were coming in from Lycée Myriam. They had started in the spring of 1997 with four girls and were now at thirty-four and climbing; in the past few days three more young women had come to the house inquiring about the workshop. The operation was thriving, and now Kamila had to face the issue that both Malika and Rahim had raised at the beginning: how to manage the number of young women who were streaming to the house each day. On any given morning as many as a dozen girls from around Khair Khana would arrive for classes, and in the afternoon another group came for the second session, just as Kamila had envisioned. In addition there were the women who came by to pick up thread and fabric for dresses they would sew in their own homes and bring back a few days later. The girls worried that their house, which was becoming a real hub for women all around the neighborhood, would attract unwanted attention. They wanted more than anything to work invisibly, but this was becoming increasingly difficult.

We need some kind of a system, Kamila thought. Otherwise, one day there will be too many girls here at once and who knows what will happen.

Her own sister's experience served as a somber reminder of what could go wrong. While still living in Karteh Parwan, Malika had run classes from her living room each morning, teaching young girls the Holy Q'uran. The lessons matched the girls' education: courses for those who knew how to read and write would focus on studying and reciting the Holy Book; girls who had not yet been in school long enough to become literate would learn reading and writing as the foundation for their study.

One day not long before moving to Khair Khana, Malika had been called away from her students to attend to a visitor, a former colleague who had arrived unexpectedly. In their teacher's absence, the girls had forgotten her oft-repeated warning to leave one by one rather than as a group, and they had poured out into the street all at once only to collide with a Taliban patrol at the end of the lane. At the neighborhood mosque that night the mullah had railed against the threat posed by Malika's school. "We know that girls are being taught in violation of our law, and this must stop at once," he had warned. Malika's husband and his cousin had insisted to the Talibs who patrolled the mosque—local men whom they had known for years—that Malika was simply teaching the Holy Q'uran. Surely the soldiers could have no objection to that, they said, since education is the duty of all Muslims. The answer they received was telling: They had no problem with her work, the soldiers insisted, and knew Malika to be a good and religious woman. They would be happy for her to continue teaching, and would even send their own daughters to her school if they could. Their bosses, however, would never allow it. She must stop her classes right away, they warned, or there would be problems for everyone. Their blunt message left no room for negotiating. Malika closed her school within a week.

Kamila thought about this story often, now that she was in the same position her sister had been in. And if it could happen to Malika—known in her neighborhood as among the most responsible and devout members of her community—it could surely happen to her.

She called Sara and the girls together to discuss the issue and come up with a solution over breakfast at seven o'clock one morning, well before their students arrived.

"Kamila, I think we need to set up a strict schedule that everyone has to stick to from now on," Laila volunteered. "We can distribute sewing supply kits to each woman on a set day every week, so that we know who is coming by when. And Saaman and I can organize the students so we don't have more than fifteen or twenty here at any one time. That's a lot, but I think we can manage it, and it's enough people to let us plow through a bunch of orders every day."

Kamila had to disguise her surprise as she listened to her sister. She was barely sixteen and she had assumed such responsibility in the past six months! "Yes, I agree;

that's a good idea," she replied. "If you and Saaman will put a schedule together for the girls, we can post it near the front door at the beginning of every week so everyone knows when they should be here."

"And we'll make it clear that no one can change her days without telling us, and that their dresses absolutely must be turned in on time," Sara added. "That will help avoid the problem we had last week when two girls brought their work later than we expected and Kamila Jan had to go back to the market with Neelab instead of Rahim. It's just too dangerous right now for us to risk that kind of thing if we can avoid it."

"While we're sitting here, I think we need to talk about space," Saaman said. "I mean the fact that we are running out of it."

Already their work had expanded from the living room into the dining room, and it was threatening to spread farther still into the last remaining family room. Dresses now hung from all sorts of unusual spaces, from doorframes and table corners to the backs of chairs. The front rooms of the family home had been transformed into a workshop that regularly ran fifteen hours a day at full capacity. Chairs forming a U filled the living room so that classes could be taught in the center and the girls could see their classmates' work, though some young women still preferred to sew sitting cross-legged on the floor. Hurricane lamps lit the rectangular room from each corner, since sunlight faded out of the sitting area in the late morning. When dusk arrived, the girls moved the lamps nearer to them, their narrow flames forming mobile orbs of light around the small sewing stations. Two zigzag machines, Kamila's first big investment in the business, sat together in a corner toward the entrance to the kitchen. They could be used only a few hours each day, when power was available. If it came on at all.

Kamila looked around and nodded in agreement. "I know," she said. "But I'm not sure how much we can do about that. I've been thinking about buying a generator from Lycée Myriam. It would be really expensive, but if we had power, we could get our work done a lot faster. All that sewing by hand takes so much time. Right now we're busy seven days a week and we're still struggling to get all our orders finished on time. Thank goodness for the students, and the fact that they are working as hard as we are!"

Most of the students were young women who lived nearby in Khair Khana and had known the Sidiqis for years. Some had attended a small class years earlier to study the Holy Q'uran, which Kamila taught while she was still in high school. That was how a number of families in the neighborhood first got to know the young teacher.

Other students, like Nasia, had come to live in Kabul after the fighting in the Shomali Plains just north of the city destroyed their families' homes and forced them to live as refugees in the capital. As soon as she heard about the school just four houses down from her uncle's home, where she and her seven siblings now lived, Nasia had pleaded with her mother to let her go. She, like many of Kamila's students, now had two jobs: during the day she sewed with the girls down the street and at night she helped her widowed mother to make chadri for shopkeepers at Lycée Myriam. Each evening the women hoped for a few hours of electricity when they would use the electric iron to press and starch the veil's blue circle of handmade, mini-accordion pleats.

And there was Mahnaz, a girl for whom Kamila's house provided a lifeline as much as a living.

She was seventeen, but her plain face and solemn manner cast a much older first impression. Her thick hands were broad and strong, which made their grace all the more surprising. Mahnaz possessed a unique gift for the delicate art of beading, but, like most of the girls who worked in the Sidiqi house, being a seamstress was not her life's aim. She had dreamed of being a professor since the age of seven.

Following the Taliban's arrival, she had stayed at home for nearly half a year, reading old school lessons and Iranian police novels, occasionally setting aside her books to join her older brothers in watching contraband Jean-Claude Van Damme movies on the family's small television. She had wanted to enroll herself in an English course that was being taught near her house, but her family worried it was too risky and forbade it.

When Mahnaz heard through a cousin's friend about Kamila and the girls her age who were sewing together just a block away, she had jumped at the opportunity to join them. Two of her sisters, one of whom was determined to become a doctor when school was allowed again, quickly decided to come along once they heard how much Mahnaz was enjoying herself. "It's not even like being in Kabul City," she told her siblings after her first day at Kamila's house. "It feels like a place where there's no Taliban at all, and no fighting. There are just all these women working together and talking and sharing stories. It's wonderful."

With so many girls learning to sew, mistakes were inevitable. Sara was now on her feet nearly all day, bustling around the room from station to station and reviewing each dress before it went out the door. "This is off, start again," she would say sternly to the girls when a dress did not measure up to her standards.

"You remind me of my father, Sara!" Kamila often joked. "I think you would have been excellent in the army!" But it was not just at work that Sara saw her role growing in importance: her small income was now contributing to her brother-in-law's kitchen and paying for the books and pencils her sons needed for school. One afternoon over lunch Sara told Kamila about her husband's oldest brother, Munir, the airplane engineer who supported their family of fifteen at home. "He was always good to us," she said as she broke off a chunk of naan from the round loaf sitting on the vinyl floor cloth in front of them, "but I knew my children and I were a problem that he had to shoulder once my husband died; it was difficult for him. Now things are much better. Two nights ago when my sister-in-law and I got up to clear the dishes after dinner he told me, 'Sara Jan, I really respect your work. Your help means a lot right now.' Kamila, this was so shocking—I mean, Munir has never been a man to talk a great deal, let alone to say such things. I couldn't even answer him properly; I just nodded and muttered, 'Thank you.'" She certainly wasn't mumbling now, Kamila thought, smiling at her friend, whose doelike brown eyes lit up as she told her story. Kamila had trouble picturing the timid and frightened woman who had shown up at her doorstep looking for work so many months earlier. I wouldn't even recognize her, she thought to herself. And I bet Sara Jan wouldn't, either.

The tailoring business was expanding rapidly, and Kamila now depended on Rahim to go to Lycée Myriam nearly every day. For marketing they always went together, but if Kamila needed only a few sewing supplies from the bazaar, Rahim would pick them up on his own after school.

For that reason Kamila didn't think anything of it

when Saaman asked her one evening if she knew where their brother was.

"It's awfully late," she said, pacing slowly around the workspace. All the students had left hours earlier, and now the girls were alone at home, working as usual.

"What time is it?" Kamila asked. "He's probably just leaving the bazaar, or maybe he ran into some friends. I'm sure he's fine."

An hour passed, and at seven she felt far less certain. He was now hours later than usual. Her stomach was churning, and she couldn't sit still.

"Did he take his bike today?" she asked the girls.

Saaman nodded yes.

Kamila dropped her work onto the floor and moved toward the door, walking up and down the small length of the foyer. Knowing that she couldn't go out and look for her brother without causing more problems made her feel even more powerless.

By now all the girls had gathered in the living room. No one spoke, no one worked. Kamila felt her eyes tearing up as she imagined how awful it would be for Rahim if her worst fears proved true. She prayed that God in his infinite mercy would keep her brother safe. He is all I have right now, Kamila thought, he and the girls. Please, please, don't take them from me. She believed it would be her fault if anything happened to Rahim since it was she who sent him to Lycée Myriam.

Finally, the gate clanged shut.

Kamila ran to her brother. He was pale and disheveled but looked unharmed.

"Oh, my goodness, what happened?" cried Laila. "Are you all right?"

"Please, please, I am fine," Rahim insisted. He hung his coat as usual, but Kamila could see something was very wrong. She sat him down at the table.

"Just tell us what happened," Kamila said, a bit more insistently than she intended. She reminded herself of Malika, the maternal enforcer who never asked but instead demanded the truth. "I'm sorry," she whispered. "We were all just so worried."

Laila hurried in with a glass of green tea, and Rahim's hands shook ever so slightly as he gratefully reached for the glass's clear handle.

"I forgot I had an extra lesson this afternoon; you know, the test preparation class?" Rahim began reluctantly. "Well, anyway, I was on my way there when I heard a noise behind me. I looked and saw there were three Talibs. I kept pedaling my bike, hoping that they would move on to someone else. I hadn't done anything wrong. But I heard their footsteps right behind me and they began yelling at me to stop. I was afraid they would catch up if I didn't, and then things would be a lot worse. So I hit my brakes.

" 'We told you to stop,' they said. 'What is your problem?' I told them I was trying to get to class, that I am a student at Khair Khana and just wanted to be at my course on time. Then they asked me how old I was, and where I was from. They wanted to see my ID card. One of them took out his *shaloq* and I kept trying to find my card, but I just couldn't remember where I had put it."

Tears were now falling down Kamila's cheeks, but she said nothing.

"Finally I found the card, but I think that just made things worse. They asked me where my father was, and if he was fighting against the Taliban. I kept telling them that Father is retired, and my family has nothing to do with politics. That we don't want any trouble. But they didn't believe me. They asked again about Father and if I had any brothers, and where were they? And then they threatened to take me to jail. I have no idea if they really were serious about it but they brought out the *shaloqs* to try to scare me. Finally another Talib came along and said there was a family that was playing a video in their house. So they got distracted and finally let me go."

The girls sat motionless, in total silence.

"Don't worry, please," he pleaded, seeing the distress on their faces. "You see I am okay. Nothing happened. It's fine."

But it was not fine; none of it was fine, Kamila thought. Next time it could be much worse.

Despite all the gains they had made—the orders from

the market, the school, the flourishing little business they had built—their lives were as precarious as everyone else's in Kabul. They were just kids trying to survive another year of war together with no parents to watch over them. All that protected them right now was their faith—and a green metal gate that kept the world outside at bay.

No, it wasn't fine at all. But the only thing Kamila could do now was to keep going. And to keep working. For all of their sakes.

# 7

# An Unexpected
# Wedding Party

The babies had been crying all night. Sleepless, overworked, and worried about the health of her twin girls, Malika was tempted to collapse onto her thick red pillow near the wooden crib and join them in their tears. But she had no time for such indulgences. The infants were feverish and colicky; as soon as it opened at 2 P.M. she would take them upstairs to Dr. Maryam's clinic.

*"Bachegak, bachegak"*—little baby, little baby—"please, I promise it will be okay," Malika whispered as she scooped both babies into a tight embrace and walked them around the room, trying to lull them to sleep. The tiny newborn twins had arrived nearly two months ahead of their due date and had struggled to gain weight and strength ever

since. They remained weak and sickly, their small bodies battling diarrhea and what seemed like an endless series of infections. Malika had been lucky to find a female doctor in time to assist her premature delivery; these days most women gave birth in their bedrooms without the benefit of professional help. Of course it wasn't guaranteed that making it to a hospital would improve an expectant mother's chances; the civil war had destroyed most medical facilities, and combatants on all sides had stripped hospitals bare of equipment and supplies. Patients had to fill their own prescriptions and even had to bring their own food.

With the Taliban in power, doctors in Kabul could once again go to work without fear of rocket attacks, but female doctors—those who hadn't fled the country when the Taliban took Kabul—faced an entirely new set of problems. The Taliban had ordered hospitals, like every other institution, to be segregated by gender, with women physicians restricted to treating female patients and working in female-only wards. They were not allowed to work with—let alone consult—their male colleagues. Foreign aid organizations were still wrestling with the question of how much support to offer the Taliban, particularly given their policies toward women, so help had been slow to reach the nation's hospitals. As a result, doctors and surgeons regularly worked without even the basics such as clean water, bandages, and antiseptics. Anesthesia was a luxury. Along with most other women in Kabul, Malika now had no choice but to seek treatment from one of the very few women doctors who had chosen to remain in the capital. Dr. Maryam, like many of her colleagues, ran a private clinic in addition to her hospital work in order to help support her family.

Malika arrived at the doctor's office early and for good reason; within thirty minutes, a crowd of women had filled the austere waiting room, with many standing against the walls holding infants in their arms. Demand for Dr. Maryam's services had grown so great in the last few months she had hired an assistant who handed out a numbered piece of paper to each woman as she entered the office. Malika waited patiently for her number to be called. She fixed her gaze on the peeling paint that curled along the old walls; she prayed for the twins' health and wondered how she would pay for whatever medicine they might need for their latest affliction.

Stepping into the treatment room at last, Malika kissed the doctor hello and stepped aside so she could begin the examination. Dr. Maryam's specialty was pediatrics, and in her presence the worried mother felt her shoulders slacken and her jaw unclench for the first time in hours. The doctor examined first one baby, then the other, with a natural confidence that came from decades of experience. As a child, Dr. Maryam had dreamt of becoming a doctor, and her parents, neither of whom had any formal education, worked relentlessly to help their daughter realize her goal. She left her rural village for college at the start of the Russian occupation, and the local Mujahideen came to Maryam's father to complain that his daughter was attending Kabul University's medical school. They suggested, rifles in hand, that a Soviet-backed school was no place for a respectable girl, and that her family must be full of sympathizers who supported the Russian invaders. In response her father made a deal: he would supply them with as much wheat as they wanted, at no charge, if they would leave his daughter alone to continue her studies. He ended up having to sell much of his family's farmland to finance Maryam's university education, but he never complained; the Mujahideen got their wheat and his daughter got her medical degree.

After completing her studies, Dr. Maryam worked for more than a decade at Kabul Women's Hospital and eventually rose to a senior position supervising its new doctors. At the same time she raised two children with her husband, a scientist by training who now owned a pharmacy not far from her clinic in Khair Khana.

Once the Taliban arrived, of course, everything changed. The new government installed its own men inside the hospital and charged them with overseeing everything that went on. They regularly burst into the women's ward to make certain that no men were present and that female doctors remained veiled while treating the sick who had come to see them. Tall in stature with a self-assured, almost regal bearing, Maryam could not easily abide being told what she could or couldn't do when it came to caring for her patients, and she found it impossible to keep her feelings to herself. She chafed at the new restrictions and voiced her frustration to her colleagues, one of whom informed upon her. Senior Taliban officials didn't take kindly to being questioned by anyone, let alone a woman, and Dr. Maryam was now regularly watched by the government's soldiers; they monitored her every move.

Despite these difficulties, Maryam maintained a schedule that impressed even Malika and Kamila. Each day she worked from 8 A.M. until 1 P.M. at the hospital before returning to Khair Khana to treat patients at her clinic, sometimes staying well into the night to see the very last woman who needed her care. Like Kamila and her sisters, she refused to turn any woman away. Most of her patients suffered from malnutrition because they couldn't afford to buy food. But depression was also running rampant, debilitating former teachers, lawyers, and civil servants who now felt powerless and full of despair, with nothing to do and nowhere to go. Many of them turned to Dr. Maryam for advice and comfort, as well as the opportunity to escape their homes.

Now, standing in her examining room with one hand around each tiny baby, the doctor turned her attention to their mother.

"I don't know who I'm more worried about, Malika:

you or your girls," she said. "Are you sleeping at all? It certainly doesn't appear so. I know you're taking care of the entire family, but you must get some rest." Her tone was calm but stern as she looked at her third patient. "You will do no one any good if you collapse."

Malika stared down at the carpet, trying to beat back the tears. She thought about her husband, her boys, her sick twins, her customers, her sisters, all the people who counted on her. In that instant she felt perfectly alone, unable to share her burden, and with no choice but to simply carry on.

"Think of all that you've done already," Maryam continued. She handed both babies to Malika and drew her chair near. "You've managed to keep your older boy in school, care for these sick little girls, help your sisters' business, and support your family. None of these are small things and you must certainly not give up now. But you have to take better care of yourself. Otherwise you will be the one I am treating next time, not the babies. Okay?"

Malika nodded wearily. She embraced the doctor in a big hug before picking up her chadri from its hook on the door and hoisting the twins into her arms once more.

"I am going to your husband's pharmacy now to fill the prescriptions," Malika said. "And you must be sure to come see me again when you and your nieces are ready for more dresses!"

Later that evening Malika confided to Kamila that

she felt better just from having had a moment of quiet to confide in someone she trusted about her problems. With dozens of young girls coming to the house every day, she and her sisters had grown much more accustomed to listening to other people's problems than to sharing their own, even with each other. Kamila had been worried about her sister for days and was relieved to hear that the doctor had insisted that she take better care of herself.

Malika, however, was not the only one to receive a lecture from Dr. Maryam. Kamila too slipped out to see her after several days of feeling sluggish and lightheaded. Maryam warned Kamila that her blood pressure was too low and she needed more rest. But following the doctor's advice was proving difficult for her, too. With orders backing up and a steady stream of new students, she was lucky to sleep more than five hours each night. Even when she finally made it to the bedroom she shared with her sisters, she stayed awake for hours worrying that they wouldn't have enough work the following week and that the girls wouldn't be able to deliver all the orders they already had.

Kamila had also taken Malika's advice and was pushing the most exceptional girls to develop their own designs and embrace their individual styles. She was finding, however, that while sewing a sample of a new dress was easy enough, churning out a dozen of them all at once required multiple trips to the fabric store and days of work from several seamstresses. Mahnaz had just dreamt up a new pattern in which an elaborate geometry of translucent beads with gold flecks at their center covered a deep purple fabric in yellow and white flowers from the neck to the waistline. Kamila was thrilled with Mahnaz's boldness and creativity, and she loved the design, but she wondered how in the world she had ever agreed to produce so many of these ornate dresses for Hamid in only seven days.

Kamila decided that if she really wanted to grow her business she would have to invest in it so that they could sew more dresses, faster. "We need machines," she said to Rahim, "and we need them now." With her faithful *mahram* at her side she went to Lycée Myriam and selected several, including an expensive embroidery apparatus imported from Pakistan and a small new generator that would go in their courtyard. The brother of one their students, Neelufar, had promised he would teach Kamila how to use the embroidery machine if she would teach his sister how to sew. Embroidered dresses sold for a premium, and those extra afghani would certainly help. "With all of this gear," she said to Rahim while he struggled to carry the whole lot back home, "there's no reason we can't triple our orders, don't you think?"

He only nodded at his sister; he was too focused on steadying the stack of machines to speak.

❊

One morning shortly after the arrival of the new equipment, Kamila was lost in her work finishing the beading on the last of Mahnaz's purple dresses. Malika sat nearby, wrestling with the folds of a pantsuit, trying to get them to lie just right. At last she noticed their young helper Neelab standing silently at her side. The small girl's eyes focused on a pile of fabric scraps on the floor while she waited for Malika to acknowledge her.

"Yes, Neelab, sorry, what is it?" she asked the girl.

"Auntie Malika, there is a family at the door—three ladies and one of them is getting married. They want to see if you can make wedding outfits for the bride."

The child looked up. "They need the dresses tomorrow."

Malika thought she had misheard. "Tomorrow?"

"Yes," the girl answered, "that's what she said."

These days the few weddings that took place were rarely rush affairs. It took too long to save or borrow the money for a celebration and gather all the guests from the far-flung places they had fled to. Anyway, most potential grooms were either outside Afghanistan or fighting on the front lines.

"Okay, ask the women to come in," Malika said. "We can see what they need."

Moments later two young women and their clearly anxious mother hurried into the room.

"Oh, thank goodness," said the older woman, looking around the crowded workshop at all the girls working and breaking into a tense smile. "This is just the kind of place we have been looking for. My name is Nabila and these are my daughters, Shafiqa and Mashal. Shafiqa is getting married the day after tomorrow and we need to get her dresses made right away. We have been driving around the city all day trying to find a female tailoring shop to take the work, but yours is the first we have found that can make what we need."

With that, Nabila pulled two bolts of fabric, one green and the other white, from a plastic tote bag.

"Here is the material," she said, handing the pile to Malika before the seamstress even had a chance to say no. "We really appreciate you getting these dresses done for us so quickly."

Malika was still a bit dumbfounded, but she smiled anyway and took the fabric.

Nabila then gestured at the younger girl, Mashal, who quickly disappeared from the room.

"Okay, yes, of course," Malika said. "We'll do it, though this kind of order would usually require at least a few days. But we've done many wedding dresses before and I think we can manage this. I'll make sure that your daughter's dresses are ready tomorrow evening."

Malika walked Shafiqa, the bride, down the hall to a makeshift tent made of pale-colored cotton sheets that served as a fitting room. She was a pretty girl of maybe nineteen or twenty, thin and a bit wan, with light eyes and high cheekbones that bisected a narrow, doll-like face. After completing Shafiqa's measurements Malika returned to the living room and found Nabila waiting for her with the other daughter, Mashal. She had apparently reappeared while the bride was getting measured and was standing, somewhat breathlessly, cradling in her arms an even larger bag than her mother's.

"I am very sorry to trouble you," the mother began, addressing Malika again. "But I see how many girls are sewing here with you and I am wondering if you would be so kind as to make four more dresses for us?" Without waiting for Malika's reply, she reached into the bag and brought out a handful of fabric. "Shafiqa's sisters and I also need gowns for the wedding party. As I said, we haven't been able to find a female tailor anywhere who could handle so many gowns at once. We are really quite desperate since the wedding is only two days away. Do you think you could make all six dresses for us?"

She passed the bag over to Malika, who was struggling to contain her amazement.

"You need two wedding dresses and four wedding party gowns made in one day?"

The woman nodded energetically. She did indeed look desperate.

Malika stood silent for a moment. This kind of order

would normally take at least a week of work. If it was even possible to get this done, which she was not at all sure of, she would need the help of all her sisters and every student in the school. It would have to be all hands on deck, starting as soon as possible. Like now.

Well, she thought to herself, we wanted more work. . . .

Malika escorted Nabila to the foyer, where she asked her to wait with the two girls, then hurried back to the living room workshop where Kamila was still absorbed in her beading.

"Kamila Jan, there is a woman here wanting me to make her six dresses in one day for her daughter's wedding party. Of course I can't do it by myself; I honestly don't even know whether we can get it done all together. It's a huge amount of work. What do you think?"

Kamila didn't need to think; she dropped the purple fabric and answered immediately and decisively.

"Yes, of course we can do it. The girls and I will help you. We're nearly finished with this order for Hamid anyway," she said. "We'll get it done—you know we always find a way. Besides, how many times have you rescued us? More times than we can count!"

"Well, it will be quite an adventure," Malika said, kissing her sister on the cheek in gratitude before returning to her new customers.

"All of you must come back today, just before six P.M.,

so your measurements can be taken," she instructed. "Usually we wouldn't ask you to come back at night because of the soldiers and the curfew, but if we're going to work quickly, we'll need your help," she said. "But please make sure not to come late; we don't want you to be on the streets or at our gate at the time of prayer."

"Yes, yes, of course, that will be fine," said the mother of the bride, now smiling. "We will see you this evening. And thank you. Thank you so much."

As soon as the women had gone, the living room began to buzz with activity as Malika called her troops to order and gave directions to each and every one.

"Okay, girls, we are going to get started on this order and we need all of your help," she began, standing before the students at the front of the living room. "We have seven hours until the women come back. By then we will need to have the shells of each dress ready for them to try on. I will lead the wedding dresses team, and Kamila will be in charge of the gowns for the mother and sisters. Saaman will cut all the fabric and do the stenciling for the embroidery. Laila and Neelab will make sure we have all the supplies we need. Sara Jan will be coming around to make sure everyone understands what they are supposed to be doing. Please don't hesitate for one second to ask any of us a question; we don't have time to make mistakes, and we are all glad to stop what we're doing and help with whatever you need. And if any of you can stay a bit later today, we would very much appreciate it."

With that, the teams broke off to begin their work. They would work in two stages, starting with the green dress, which Shafiqa would wear during the ceremony in which the bride and groom consented to marriage. Then she and the girls would turn to the white gown, which Shafiqa would wear to greet her guests during the wedding reception afterward. The bride had requested that both frocks be very long and very plain, with only a bare minimum of beading around the neckline and sleeves. It struck Malika as a bit odd, particularly since the bride had seen from the dresses hanging around the workspace what pretty embroidery work the girls could do. "But so much the better," she told the girls. "The handwork would have set us back at least half a day."

Kamila's group of seamstresses began by unrolling the fabric Nabila had brought and matching each material with the woman who would wear it. She wrote their names on a piece of scrap paper that she then taped to the floor next to each pile of fabric. Once Saaman had cut the material and drawn the patterns for them, the girls went to work in pairs, dividing each bodice and skirt into panels that they could work on separately. When it came time to work on the sleeves, the girls wrote down each customer's arm length and placed it on the table in front of them before starting to run stitches across the top of the fabric in the way that Kamila had taught them. This would make it easier to attach the arms to the rest of the dress later on. The girls made certain to leave extra fabric for the first fitting. As their teachers had told them so many times, it's better for a sleeve to be too long than too short. "Long," the mantra went, "you can always shorten."

The room hummed with activity but there was little noise aside from the whirrs and clicks of the sewing machines alongside the purr of the generator and the directions that Malika and Kamila called out every few minutes. Everyone was focused on the job before her. After an hour or so, one of the younger students asked Kamila if she might play a cassette she had brought, promising to keep the volume low. Kamila agreed it would be nice to have some music, and she reached into a cabinet to retrieve her father's old Chinese tape recorder. Soon the room filled with the melodic voice of Farhad Darya, a legendary folk-pop artist and former Kabul University music teacher who had been named Radio Afghanistan's "Singer of the Year" in 1990, the same year he fled Kabul for Europe after running afoul of the Soviet-backed Afghan government. The girls knew all the words to every ballad, and they sang along quietly to the tunes as they sewed.

When the bodice of the white wedding dress had begun to take shape and the skirt was almost finished, Malika asked one of the students whose height nearly matched the bride's to come and stand in the middle of the room. Here

Malika's experience showed as she pinned the front and back sections of each dress around the girl and took quick stock of how much work lay ahead.

"Okay, this is a good start," Malika said. "On the skirts, make sure we have a cushion of fabric at the bottom. Remember they are straight skirts, which can be tricky with the shiny white fabric, so go slowly and leave yourself a lot of room to work. Our bride will be back before long."

Once she had finished gathering all the fabric and laying out the zippers and clasps they would need later on, Laila went to the kitchen to prepare a tray of chai and *halwaua-e-aurd-e-sujee*, a sweet confection of flour, sugar, oil, and nuts, for the girls to snack on. The dinner hour was approaching, and it was clear she would need to make enough food for at least twenty, not the usual twelve she normally cooked for. She sent Neelab to the store across the street to buy more naan and onions. Rice they purchased in large sacks and it looked like they had enough for now; no need to buy anything before they must.

At 6 P.M. sharp the bridal party rattled the gate and knocked at the girls' front door once more. They warmly greeted Malika and Kamila and followed them to the fitting room. Stepping gingerly into her bridal dress to avoid being pinched by the straight pins that now held the panels together, Shafiqa stood motionless while Malika and Kamila walked around her, exchanging ideas with one another and taking notes about which places needed to be taken in and which needed to be let out. Afterward Nabila and her other daughters each had her turn. Kamila made certain that the young students were managing the fittings they had been assigned to, and she found herself filled with pride. Soon they won't even need me, she thought to herself, marveling at how much the girls had learned and how confidently they worked with their customers.

Before the women left, Nabila stopped at the door to arrange her chadri. "I know this is a big job for you and all your students," she said to Malika. "My family and I are very grateful. We haven't had so many happy occasions these last few years, and this is one we're glad to celebrate."

"This is our work and we're glad to do it," Malika said, smiling. "We'll look forward to seeing you and your daughters again tomorrow morning for your last fitting. Please come early so we have as much time as possible."

Malika, Kamila, and their teams toiled on into the night. Rahim, too, joined in the dressmaking marathon once he had returned from school; his sisters were eager to have his embroidery and beading expertise. All of them would indeed have to work around the clock, as Malika had predicted. Sometime after midnight, the young women finally called an end to the day. The sisters would rise for prayer at dawn and pick up where they left off. All of them were exhausted, though Kamila still had enough energy to tease her younger sister.

"I don't think we'll do this again," she said, extinguishing the last of the hurricane lamps. "When you get married, Saaman, I insist on at least two months' notice."

"Kamila Jan," her sister retorted, "by the time I get married we won't have this business anymore; you'll be teaching literature to a classroom full of students and who knows what I'll be doing but one thing I'm certain of: we won't have time to make dresses; we'll go to the finest store and buy them!"

Early the next morning the girls were back at their machines.

When Nabila and her daughters returned, they found the dressmakers so occupied with their gowns that they barely noticed the bridal party entering the house. This time Shafiqa could try on her dress without fear since Malika had removed the last of the pins. She had finished sewing the gown together just an hour earlier.

"It is so beautiful," Shafiqa said, taking a step forward, then completing a quick pirouette. "The neckline is perfect, and the beading is lovely."

"You look very pretty," said Kamila. "We hope you will have a wonderful wedding."

The green dress was almost finished as well. Mahnaz just needed to complete the last of the beading, which she rushed off to do now that they knew Shafiqa was happy with the dress's design and pleased with its fit.

"I think we are in fine shape," Malika told Kamila later that afternoon. "We should be ready by the time they return this evening to pick everything up. We just need to focus on finishing the dresses for Nabila and her daughters, and those gowns are so much simpler."

But they did not have the luxury of time. Hours before they were expected, Nabila and her daughters were once again at the girls' doorstep.

This time they were really in a hurry.

"Do you have the dresses ready, Malika Jan?" Nabila pleaded as she rushed into the workspace. Her daughters, including the bride-to-be, stood in a close huddle behind her, watching nervously. "I am so sorry. We have had a change of plans and we need the gowns right away."

If Malika was stunned she didn't show it. After years of sewing for friends and neighbors she had grown accustomed to the most impossible requests and had taught herself to answer calmly and patiently.

"We have most of them," she responded, stealing a look at her sister, "but we're still finishing your gown." Kamila marveled at her sister's composure. "We'll have it done in just a few more minutes. Please sit down and have some tea while you wait."

"Please, I don't care about my dress, don't let that hold us up," Nabila insisted. The pitch of her voice was moving upward fast. "We really are in a hurry."

Malika took a breath.

"Okay, wait here," she said, motioning to the pillows in their workspace. "We're just finishing the hem on your dress and we need only five minutes to get it done. Then you can take everything."

Her words unleashed a torrent of activity as the girls pulled the white and green frocks down from the doorway where they hung. Since the power was out and they had used the last of their generator fuel, Nasia and Neelufar went to the kitchen and lit the gas stove that they would use to heat the steam iron. Malika refused to let Shafiqa's gowns leave her house without a proper pressing. No bride wants a wrinkled wedding dress.

As for Nabila's gown, Sara was directing the students to focus on finishing it, not perfecting it. One of the girls stood still in the gray patterned garment while three others crouched around her on the floor sewing the hem.

And then, finally, "We're done!" one of the girls yelled to Sara, still clenching a needle between her teeth. The trio had finished its work. By now the other five dresses were pressed and packed, waiting by the door for Neelab and Malika's son Hossein to help their anxious owners carry them outside.

Malika hurried over to give the last garment a final check. "It looks good, girls. With more time we could have made it even better, but this will do."

By now Nabila had risen from her seat to pace across

the workshop. As soon as she saw her dress being placed in the bag, she offered hasty hugs to Malika and Kamila, profusely thanking them for all of their help while at the same time commanding her daughters to get moving: they had to go now.

Neelab picked up the package with great care and accompanied the women through the courtyard to the street outside. There she found the day's biggest surprise.

Neelab saw three cars waiting in the street for the women. She had to catch herself from exclaiming out loud when she realized that two of them were dark Toyota Hilux trucks with Q'uranic verses painted on the side. Taliban vehicles.

Several Talibs were sitting in the first truck and to Neelab's surprise they were exceedingly polite. They gratefully took the package of dresses from her and, even more, handed her a bit more than the five hundred thousand afghani she had requested, per Malika's agreement with the mother of the bride, Nabila. In the second truck sat a young Talib whom Neelab guessed to be the groom. Behind him was the Toyota Corolla that would transport Shafiqa, her mother, and sisters to the wedding. No flowers or streamers adorned the car's hood and front bumper as they would have in the old days, before the Taliban put an end to noisy celebrations. But Neelab had no doubt whatsoever that this was indeed the start of a wedding procession.

Kamila and Malika looked at one another in amazement after Neelab had finished her story. And then they broke out in huge smiles. The dresses they had just dedicated the last thirty hours to making were about to be worn in a Taliban wedding. "Oh Malika," Kamila said, "that's why the gowns had to be so simple!"

"Maybe the groom had to leave for the front and that was why they were in such a hurry?" Laila added.

Hours later Malika was still rewinding the events of the last two days in her head. "I just don't believe it," she said. She was now sitting cross-legged on the floor, having stopped moving for the first time all day to enjoy a cup of tea and a plate of spaghetti.

Kamila grinned.

"This is good news," she said. "At least we know some of the Taliban like our work!"

The event confirmed what Kamila and Malika had long suspected: Taliban outside Khair Khana now knew about their operation, both Kamila's school and Malika's made-to-measure business. And so far, not only were the soldiers not shutting down their ventures, they were quietly supporting them.

Kamila had known for some time that this was the case when it came to local Talibs who served at the lowest levels of government, far from the decision makers in Kandahar. A few months earlier, two sisters had come to her asking to join her courses. Kamila knew their family well; they were Pashtuns from the south who had lived for many years in Khair Khana, just behind the Sidiqis and next to the neighborhood mosque. The girls' uncle was a good friend of Najeeb's. Kamila had heard a while back that Mustafa, the girls' father, was now working with the Taliban. He patrolled Khair Khana with minimal force, using his relationships with his neighbors to try to keep their corner of Kabul from attracting his bosses' notice. Kamila had told the sisters that she would be happy to have them join the school. She was eager to help her brother's friends, and besides, she thought, she was glad to have their father on her side. Not long afterward, the oldest of the two girls, Masuda, had asked her teacher if she could speak with her in private, away from the other students.

"My father has asked me to pass along a message," she said, tightly gripping her sewing kit. "He asked me to please tell Kamila Jan that I know that she has a business, and that I also know she is an honorable woman whose work is helping families in Khair Khana. She should please be careful to make certain that no men come to the house, ever. If she follows the rules and if she makes sure that only women are working with her, she should not have any problems. Tell her that I will try to let her know if any of my bosses are asking about her business or planning to come to her house."

From the way that Masuda had recited her father's

words, gazing upward as if trying to pry open the pages of an invisible notebook, Kamila could see that she had worked hard to memorize his message without missing a word. The importance of what he shared had not been lost on her, despite her youth.

"Please tell him my sisters and I very much appreciate his help," Kamila replied, taking Masuda's hands in her own. "We will do everything we can to follow his advice."

As the weeks went by and their operation grew, Kamila was sure that the Taliban must be asking about her business at the mosque, just as they had with Malika's school. She gave thanks every day that so far she had heard nothing from the government's men.

She would do all she could to keep it that way.

# 8

# A New
# Opportunity Knocks

Evening arrived and with it came electricity along Khair Khana's main road. The girls rushed to plug in the sewing machines and make the most of the power for as long as it lasted. Sewing well into the evening, they interrupted the whirrs and clacks of their machines only to flip on the BBC's nightly news program. More fighting in the north was the headline, but that was hardly new. The Taliban may have brought security to the streets of Kabul, but peace remained elusive.

Suddenly the girls heard the front gate creak open. They sprang to their feet and looked at one another in alarm, the machines now bobbing up and down on their own without hands to guide them. Kamila's heart beat in her ears. Who would have a key? she wondered. And who in the world would come this late at night? It was just before nine.

"I'll go see . . . ," said Kamila.

She dropped the dress she was hemming, grabbed a dark scarf that hung on the rack near the door, and stepped into the courtyard. She could hear Saaman right behind her and Laila yelling for Rahim back inside.

A dark figure, thin and tall, moved toward her. Standing still in the chill autumn air she cried out the words that set her sisters at ease:

"Father, it's you!"

In relief and joy she rushed to embrace him, nearly leaping into his long arms as she had so often when she was a girl. "Oh, we are so happy to see you," she said, helping him through the front door. "You must be hungry—it must have taken you hours to get here."

"Yes," he replied, "there are checkpoints everywhere and almost all the paths into the city are blocked." He stopped and gave her a look she knew well: forgiving if also a bit stern. "It's not easy getting in or out of Parwan." Then, the glower softening into smile: "As you know."

She nodded. Just a month earlier she had visited Parwan, braving the Taliban and Northern Alliance checkpoints and hours of travel by bus and on foot with her nephew Adel. At ten years of age he was old enough to serve as a *mahram* but too young to attract attention from the soldiers. The two had started out before five o'clock that morning on a ramshackle bus that took them out of Kabul through Taliban territory. After clearing the first checkpoint they continued on to Dornama, a small district at the foot of the Hindu Kush mountains. Kamila and her companion then trudged for more than six hours through the high mountain pass, at the other end of which they at last caught another bus, which took them along the bumpy road to Gulbahar.

"What are you doing here?" Mr. Sidiqi had demanded when he opened the door and found the bedraggled travelers. His voice bore the sharp tone of a senior military officer who would brook not even the slightest opposition. "Don't you know how dangerous it is to travel now?"

His anger took Kamila aback, and she barely managed to mumble a reply.

"We . . . we just came to see you and Mother. The girls and I have been so worried about you both, so we thought that Adel and I would come to make sure that everything is okay." Kamila had dared to make the journey so she could bring her parents some of the money the girls had earned from their sewing business in Khair Khana—"just in case you need anything."

"Kamila Jan, that is foolish," Mr. Sidiqi said. "A young girl like you traveling by yourself and taking such risks? Anything could happen. You know that. I appreciate your support of the family, but you must listen to me and promise not to come again. Don't worry about your mother and me. We will be fine so long as we know all of you are safe there in Kabul."

He made her promise to leave the very next day, but meanwhile, the family would have a joyous evening together. Cousins and friends from around the neighborhood came for dinner to catch up on all the news and hear about what was happening in Kabul. As luck would have it one of the cousins knew of a group that was leaving for the city at dawn. Mr. Sidiqi announced that Kamila and her small companion would be happy to join them.

And so once again they were up with the sun, for the long trek home. After a two-hour bus ride through Parwan, they followed the long trail of women and a few older men, retracing their steps across the mountain pass and occasionally struggling to share the trail with the donkeys and horses that were carrying more fortunate travelers. The nylon chadri trapped the sticky daytime heat with unrelenting efficiency, and Kamila watched enviously as the older ladies in the group pulled back their veils to see better as they navigated the uneven terrain. As a young woman, Kamila knew she was a target for fighters on both sides of the conflict, as well as bandits who were out only for themselves. So she kept her face covered, holding the slippery chadri in place with her hands while rivers of sweat streamed down her face.

But all of that seemed like ages ago. Tonight it was her father who had dared to make the treacherous daylong journey from the north. Kamila gave thanks to Allah for having protected him along the way, but she worried that if her father was here, something must be the matter. She knew he would never leave Parwan otherwise.

Hurrying to help him onto a pillow in the living room, the younger girls brought him a cup of tea and immediately began a barrage of questions. How is Mother? What is going on in Parwan? How much fighting is there? How long will you stay? Did you see all the dresses hanging in the living room?

"Girls," he interrupted, smiling, "I'm very glad to see all of you. And yes, of course I see that you have quite a workshop here!"

He stopped a moment, looking at each of them, and turned serious.

"I know things are very difficult for you all. You miss your classes and your friends and you've had to put all your plans for the future on hold. But you are doing such great work for the family and also for this community. It makes me very proud. One day, Inshallah, we will have peace. Schools will be open and we'll all be together again. But for now, you must continue to sew and listen to your sisters and learn as best you can. I know that you will."

"Yes, we will, Father," said Laila; she was the only one who spoke.

"And now," he said, his narrow face widening into a

playful grin, "we are all going to have a nice dinner, and then I am going to speak with Kamila Jan for a while."

Following a meal of rice, naan, and potatoes, with a bit of meat to celebrate the special occasion of his visit, Kamila and her father sat by themselves in a corner of the living room. He barely recognized it, what with all the hanging fabric and the machines that took up every last bit of space. It was late and the electricity was long gone, so Kamila lit a gas lamp.

"Kamila Jan," he began, "tomorrow I am going to Iran to stay with Najeeb. The fighting is getting too close and it's just too dangerous for me to stay. The Taliban are looking for anyone who they think has supported Massoud, and they've started asking all of our neighbors about me. It's better for all of us if I'm out of the country."

Knowing how much her father loved Afghanistan, Kamila couldn't imagine how difficult it was for him to finally decide to leave. He had never had to flee his own land before, no matter how bad things had gotten. "There's just no role for me here anymore; I can't work and the fighting is destroying everything in the north." Ever the soldier, he betrayed little of the emotion Kamila was certain he must be feeling. "I want you to know I'm proud of you. I never for one moment doubted that you would be able to take care of our family and that you could do anything you set your mind to. You must stay at it, and you must try as hard as you can to help others. This is our country and we must stay and see it through whatever comes. That is our obligation and our privilege. If you need anything at all while I am away, send me a message and I will be there. Okay?"

Kamila promised her father she would. She had no right to feel sorry for herself, she thought. At least her family had managed to stay safe so far, and their business was earning enough to keep everyone fed and cared for. Her job was to get on with her work. Her father's words reminded her of that. Still, it would be difficult to know that he was so far away. And she knew how dangerous a journey he still faced.

Early the next morning he set off for Iran. Kamila sent with him an envelope that contained a letter for Najeeb and as much money as she could afford to give them.

Only a few weeks after he left, Mrs. Sidiqi arrived. Before he had departed from Khair Khana, Mr. Sidiqi had instructed Rahim to return to Parwan and bring his mother back to the capital, where she could live with her children rather than remain alone in the north.

Kamila was struck by how tired she looked. The trip to Kabul was hard enough to exhaust a teenager, let alone a woman in her late forties who had suffered from heart problems since the birth of her eleventh child. And she must have worried for weeks about her husband's safety. Her gray braids hung loosely from their tight rows and her breath came in short, labored intervals. While the younger girls raced to roll out a mattress for her to rest on, Malika and Kamila served tea and warm bread. Kamila recounted how Malika had arrived several months earlier and helped get the business started, teaching the sisters everything that their mother had taught her back in high school.

When Kamila awoke the next morning, she found her mother already out of bed and hard at work making breakfast. How she had managed to get up before any of them, Kamila could not imagine, since it was barely seven. After washing and saying her prayers, Kamila entered the kitchen to find water already boiling on the small gas stove and toasted naan sitting on the counter. It had been a long time since she and her siblings had had their parents with them.

As they shared their tea, the girls told her the story of a wedding they had just attended in Kabul for their cousin Reyhanna. Any such celebration was a marketing opportunity for their business now, and the girls had designed four stunning new dresses for the occasion. Unlike the traditional clothes they made for the stores at Lycée Myriam or Mandawi Bazaar, the gowns they wore to the wedding dinner were both modern and stylish, designed with Kabul girls in mind—as much as the new rules would allow, anyway. Malika's had been light blue with a navy and gold beaded waistline and full sleeves that reached to the wrist, while Kamila's had been red with small and finely embroidered flowers ringing the sleeves and the neckline. After the wedding, their teenage cousins and a handful of the bride's friends had flocked to place orders for similar gowns. Laila told her mother that they were planning to make a new round of dresses in preparation for Eid al-Adha, the holiday commemorating the prophet Abraham's devotion to Allah. Though they themselves were on their own in the capital and had few visits to make, the girls' students and their parents now came to offer their respects during the holiday. The sisters in Khair Khana had become as much their family as any relative still living in Kabul.

After everyone had eaten and Rahim had put on his turban and headed off to school, Kamila and her sisters gave their mother a full tour of the workspace. Laila showed her the schedule she had created and described how Saaman would cut the long bolts of fabric for the seamstresses and get the material ready for the sewing, stenciling, beading, and embroidery that followed. With particular pride Kamila told her mother how Rahim had become an expert tailor and how Laila was helping manage not just the operations of the business but also the menu, since she helped prepare the girls' lunch each day.

As the morning wore on, the students soon began to arrive, one by one. Mrs. Sidiqi made sure to greet each of them. As she expected, she knew many of the young women's families; she asked after their parents and attentively listened to the stories of their hardships, silently shaking her head in sympathy and concern. Several of the girls seemed grateful to have someone they could trust outside their own family to discuss their problems with. One young woman explained that her mother, a widow, received the green ration cards from the United Nations' World Food Program to buy subsidized bread from the bakery nearby, but the help was hardly enough to feed a family of eight. That is why she needed the money she earned from her sewing, plus whatever her little brother earned selling candy on the street.

Mrs. Sidiqi listened to each of the young women and comforted them as best she could, reminding them how much they had already survived and assuring them that things would get better eventually. "Don't forget your school lessons," she urged them; "you don't want to fall far behind when classes begin again." In the meantime, she encouraged the girls to consider her home as their own and to help one another to get through the difficult times.

Saaman and Laila taught the morning's sewing classes while Mrs. Sidiqi sat toward the back of her living room looking on. She told Kamila later that she was deeply impressed to see how much the girls had grown up while she and their father had been away. Kamila, she said, must work with Malika to keep the family going now that her father was abroad. No matter what happened, she said, they must stay together and remain in their home. God would keep them safe if it was his will.

A few weeks later she returned to Parwan amid promises to return again soon.

❁

Again the girls were on their own, and the fighting around them intensified. It was 1998, and the end of summer saw the northern city of Mazar-e-Sharif fall to the Taliban once more, handing the new government a significant victory amid allegations of brutality on all sides that went beyond the usual wartime bloodshed to which they were all so accustomed. In Kabul, rocket attacks came at unexpected intervals, and the noose continued to tighten around the lives of families all over the city, particularly for the women. The Taliban decreed that women must be treated at female-only hospitals, but most of these had closed due to either a lack of supplies or of doctors. The one that remained open struggled to find beds for its patients, whom it cared for without the benefits of clean water, IV fluids, or functioning X-ray machines. With autumn came a frigid cold that threatened the desperate city with starvation, along with a cholera epidemic. Relief programs funded by the UN and other organizations tried to get wheat, oil, and bread to those who were worst off, but the need swamped anything that a single agency was capable of providing. Drinkable water was in short supply, and few families had much of anything left to sell.

Kamila and Rahim visited markets around the city at least twice a week, regularly returning to the Shar-e-Naw neighborhood to meet new shopkeepers whom people they trusted had told them about or introduced them to. When the siblings took the bus, Kamila noticed that the talk among the women in the back was all about who was making what handicraft at home, which store owners were buying which goods, and how much a shopkeeper would pay for this or that item. "Everyone seems to have become an entrepreneur," Kamila observed, astonished by how much had changed. Before the Taliban, women had spent their bus rides discussing work or school or the latest government intrigue. Now they seemed to speak only of marketing and business.

Arriving home from the old city's Mandawi Bazaar with Rahim one gray and chilly afternoon, Kamila was surprised to find two women sitting in her living room warming up near the wooden heater. The ladies had stopped by the day before at the urging of Kamila's cousin Rukhsana, who had told them about Kamila's small business and suggested they see her work for themselves. They worked with Rukhsana at UN Habitat, formally known as the UN Centre for Human Settlements, and they were in Kabul recruiting women for a project that was just now expanding. The pair had spent their first afternoon at

Kamila's asking all about the girls' operation: how many women were working with the sisters, how they found markets for their goods, and how their apprentice program worked.

Kamila wondered why her esteemed guests had decided to stop in again so soon. She had great respect for the work of the two ladies, Mahbooba, a sturdy woman with thin eyebrows and a no-nonsense demeanor, and Hafiza, a quite handsome woman with curly dark hair that fell around her shoulders. Hafiza had mentioned to Kamila that she was a scientist by training, and it showed; she had a cerebral seriousness that commanded Kamila's attention. Surrounding the important visitors and dangling from every available perch in the sitting room/workshop were dozens of wedding dresses for a large order Saaman was in the middle of completing. The gowns were to go to Mazar in the morning with Hassan, another of Ali's older brothers, who would sell them to shopkeepers in the northern city eager for bridal inventory.

Kamila bounded into the room and warmly embraced both her visitors, asking about their families and welcoming them to her home. Laila brought a snack of sweets and special butter cookies that the girls enjoyed only on special occasions, and finally Mahbooba began to speak. She described to her young host the work she did with UN Habitat, which was why she was here today. Kamila had first heard about Habitat during the civil war when the agency stepped in to repair some of Kabul's ruined water systems. Several years later, her cousin Rahela, Rukhsana's older sister, had joined the organization at the urging of its energetic new leader in Mazar-e-Sharif, Samantha Reynolds.

A tenacious Englishwoman who was not yet thirty, Samantha had succeeded in engaging women for the first time in the process of identifying and solving the city's vast infrastructure problems. Prior to her arrival at the UN, women had been routinely ignored during community consultations, remaining inside while their husbands, fathers, and sons went to the mosque to meet with international donors and tell them which water, sewage, and waste removal projects mattered most to the neighborhood.

Samantha recruited Rahela to join her in changing that equation, with backing from the city's mullahs. Together they helped communities tackle their own local sanitation and infrastructure problems and start neighborhood schools and health clinics for women and girls. The last Kamila had heard, Rahela had enlisted Rukhsana to grow what were now known as the Women's Community Forums where people—where women—gathered to take part in jobs and social programs they designed, supported, and supervised. Most of the profits the women earned from their work were plowed back into the forums to fund more grassroots projects. Mahbooba explained that she had only recently returned to Kabul from Mazar, where she had found safety after leaving her Kabul University teaching position during the civil war. For the last few years she had helped Samantha and Rahela establish Women's Forums in the north, and now they had gotten funding to expand the program.

"Kamila," she said, pointing at the dresses and machines around the room, "Rukhsana told us about your business, but even she didn't know it had grown so much. We were looking around yesterday and today before you came home, and we saw all the bustle and all the girls sewing here. Your sisters Saaman and Laila told us a little bit about the contracts you have and how the classes work. It's very impressive that you've managed to do so much—and without running into problems with the Taliban."

Kamila blushed in gratitude, and explained that she wanted to keep growing the business, even though it was getting harder to find new shopkeepers who would place orders. "I'm starting to realize that we're just never going to have enough work for all of the women who come here looking for jobs."

"That is why we're here," Mahbooba replied. "You know about the Community Forums from Rahela Jan and Rukhsana's work, I believe. Well, we opened the first few forums here in Kabul about a year ago, and now we're in the process of starting several more around the city.

District Ten will open soon and we want you to come and be part of it. We need girls like you with real experience in business."

Kamila sat perfectly still, her nearly full glass of green tea now cold. A rush of questions flooded her mind.

"May I ask: How are you even opening forums here now?" she began. "I thought it was illegal to work with foreigners or foreign organizations. How is the UN still hiring women? I heard that all their female employees had either gone to Pakistan or been sent home."

It was Hafiza, the scientist, who answered. "Anne, the Frenchwoman who manages the Community Forums here in Kabul, meets frequently with the Ministry of Social Affairs and has kept good relations with them, so we've been able to get permission to expand our forums. And Rahela has been negotiating with the local Taliban ministries nonstop to keep the centers in Mazar open. We have great support from the community, which is the biggest reason that we've been able to continue our work. Otherwise we would have had to stop a long time ago. At the moment the forums here in Kabul are more or less permitted since only women meet there and they're offering small income-generation programs. And with the help of a neighborhood mullah we even received Taliban approval for girls to attend classes at one of the men's forums, so you see that some local commanders can be convinced of the value of our work. In any event, the

forums officially belong to the Community Fora Development Organization, which is an Afghan organization, not a foreign one, so the restrictions don't exactly
apply. Of course the rules change nearly every day, so
some weeks require far more cleverness than others to
keep things going. But, as you know, there's always a way
when the need is so great."

Kamila nodded. There was indeed.

"But what exactly can you still do here in Kabul?" she
asked the two women. "And where are you holding your
programs? Surely you're not permitted to have offices?"

"Oh, no, that's impossible now," Hafiza confirmed.
"The forums usually operate out of people's homes or
houses that neighborhood women rent specifically for the
program. That makes it easier for the forum to be a part
of the community and also enables them to move locations
quickly if problems arise."

Mahbooba picked up her colleague's thread: "As for
the specific programs we're running here, they usually fall
into three categories—but you will learn more about this
during your training, of course."

Kamila let out a small laugh. She loved meeting women
who were as dogged as she.

"First, there is education. Right now a few hundred
students, mostly girls, but boys as well, are learning in
our schools, where we teach in two sessions each day. We
study the Holy Q'uran, which gives us some protection in

the event the Taliban come to see us, as well as Dari and mathematics. For older women, we hold literacy courses.

"Then we offer services. Some of the forums run small clinics that offer basic medical care to women and teach things like health and hygiene. We also have a kitchen garden program that teaches women how to grow tomatoes and lettuce so they can provide food and better nutrition for their families.

"And then there's the production section, where we think your experience will be most helpful. The forums provide sewing, carpet weaving, and knitting supplies, and women receive money for the clothing, blankets, and carpets they make. It's not very much, but it's something, and almost as important, it gives the women work to do for the income we give them. They're very reluctant to take our help otherwise, you know, since they don't want handouts. We're also setting up a shop at the UN guesthouse to sell the women's goods to the foreigners who stay there. And of course we'd love to have your ideas as well."

Kamila's mind was racing with new business ideas for the forums. Surely she could help market the crafts and clothes the women were making, even if they were too simple for the shops at Lycée Myriam. The work sounded important—and exciting. Kamila was beginning to see what the next step might be for her, after the sewing school and the tailoring business: something even larger, where she could help many more women.

When Mahbooba asked, "Will you join us?" Kamila didn't have to think about her answer. "Oh, yes," she replied. "I'm definitely interested." But she paused for a moment, then added, "I have to speak with my sisters first. I'm not sure how Malika Jan will feel about it since we already have so much work here at home."

Mahbooba heard the hesitation in Kamila's voice; she knew from Kamila's cousin Rukhsana that Malika was the eldest in the house now, and that Kamila would need to defer to her will. She ramped up her pitch.

"Kamila Jan, of course there are risks, but this program is really making a difference. It's almost all that's left out there for women now; you know that. When we announce that we're starting an income-generation program for one hundred people, do you know how many women show up to wait in line for hours, even on the coldest days of winter? Four hundred, sometimes five hundred. Each winter we run emergency relief programs and we cannot even come close to meeting the enormity of the need. Not one woman we've spoken with has yet said no to working with us. I know from your cousin and I can see from your work that you are not one to turn down an opportunity to serve our community and to share all the business skills you've learned."

Kamila assured the women that she would take to heart everything they had said and that she considered it an honor even to be considered for such a post with so prestigious an organization. After all, she was just a girl from Khair Khana and here was a chance to be part of a program led by professionals in Japan and Switzerland and the United States, at a time when her country was entirely cut off from the rest of the world.

"I promise I'll get back to you in just a few days," she told her visitors as she helped them on with their coats and chadri and walked them to her gate. "Thank you for coming."

As soon as they had left, Kamila collapsed on a pillow to think about everything the women had said. She was amazed that Habitat was managing to create opportunities at a time when it seemed that every door for women was closing. And she couldn't imagine saying no to this chance, given the miserable state of her city. Besides, wasn't this exactly what she and her father had discussed only weeks ago—helping as many people as she could? Didn't she have his blessing to do precisely this sort of work? She knew she could learn so much from the women who ran the forums and the foreigners who led Habitat. And surely she would make connections in this new job that would only help her family. With her cousins already working there, Malika and her parents couldn't raise too many objections, could they?

Later that evening, just after dinner, Kamila went to find her older sister to tell her all about what had happened that afternoon.

She found Malika still at work, sitting next to her babies' wooden crib sewing a seam on a burgundy dress that Kamila had been admiring for days.

"That is just so beautiful," she said. "I'm ready to order one for myself!"

"Thank you," said Malika, looking up at her sister and laughing. "How are you? We haven't spoken all day; it's been so busy!"

"Malika Jan," Kamila began, "there's something I want to discuss with you—it's about the visit we had today from Rahela and Rukhsana's colleagues, Mahbooba and Hafiza. They are working here with UN Habitat; you know, the group Rahela works with in the north? Anyway, they are starting a new Community Forum in Kabul that will offer classes for girls and jobs programs for women."

Kamila paused for a moment and took a breath in, aware that her sister was no longer smiling.

"They want me to join them," she went on. "I would help with home business projects like sewing and knitting and carpet making. It's a bit like what we've been doing here, but on a smaller scale."

Kamila's hopes that her sister would be as thrilled as she was to hear the news were quickly dashed; it was clear from Malika's face that she was anything but. Malika stared at the wall beyond Kamila and inhaled deeply, trying to calm her nerves the way she did whenever she was upset.

"Are you serious about this, Kamila Jan?" she asked. She spoke in a low and carefully controlled tone of pained disappointment. Kamila could tell that her sister was trying to hold back her anger, but she feared Malika was on the verging of losing it as her voice began to rise. "Do you know the punishment for girls who get caught working with foreigners? They get thrown in prison, or even worse. Do you know that? What could you possibly be thinking?"

Kamila answered in a measured and respectful tone, hoping to cool her sister's ire. She did not want to fight with her about this, but she had no intention of giving in. It was like her fight to attend Sayed Jamaluddin during the civil war all over again.

"Malika Jan, this is important," she said. "This is an opportunity to support a lot of women, women who have no place else to turn." Kamila paused for a second, marshaling the points in her argument.

"And it's a chance for me and for our family. I need to learn more and I want to work with professional people. I have to think about my future. I was never meant to be a tailor; you know that. It's the business and the management that I'm good at, that I really enjoy."

Kamila's short speech only made Malika more unhappy. She saw now that her younger sister was determined to go forward with this mad idea, and Malika was willing to do anything she could to stop her.

"Kamila Jan, if it's money you need, we have it," Malika said. "Our family is doing okay; we have plenty of work. I'll make sure that you get whatever it is that you want. But you cannot take this job. If something happens, I am responsible for you. Our parents are not here and it will be on my head. We don't need your salary and we definitely don't need the problems this job will surely bring."

Kamila started to answer, but her sister wasn't finished. Her face flushed with indignation.

"What do you think will happen to me, to your other sisters, if you are caught? And to my husband, the father of these twins? They punish the men in the family, too, you know. Are you willing to put all of us at risk? In the name of your family and all that is sacred"—she finished by pleading to Kamila with words that forbade defiance— "do not take this job."

For a moment they sat in silence, locked in their unhappy standoff. Kamila hated that she had upset someone she loved so dearly, but Malika's opposition had only toughened Kamila's resolve by showing her the stakes of this decision. Her life was about more than her own safety.

"I have to," Kamila said, looking down at the floor, and then at the twins, anywhere but at her sister. She just could not believe that Malika, who had supported her through every trial she had faced for the past twenty-one years, was refusing to back her now. "God will help me because I am going to help my community. I put my life in the hands of Allah and I am sure he will keep me safe because this is work for his people. I must do this. I hope you'll understand one day."

She was halfway out of the room before she offered the final words of the conversation—heated ones she immediately regretted.

"If something does happen to me, I promise I will not come to you to get me out of it," she said. "It will be my responsibility."

❋

One week later, Kamila began working in District 10's Community Forum. Her salary was ten dollars a month. Kamila studied her Habitat leaflets every night and committed to memory Habitat's founding principles about the importance of leadership, consensus, and transparency. She also received her first formal lessons in bookkeeping. Habitat closely tracked the $9,900 that the UN provided to fund each new forum, and one of Kamila's tasks was to help detail how every production section dollar had been spent.

In time, Kamila herself began to teach a class on the Holy Q'uran in addition to her work running tailoring programs for women. Each morning, packs of students tiptoed excitedly through the foyer, working hard not to succumb to their enthusiasm and break the rules with loud shouts or giggles. It had stunned Kamila to hear through the Khair Khana grapevine that several Afghan girls she knew who had fled to Pakistan had lost interest in their studies. Now that it had been taken away, Kabuli girls of every age understood exactly how precious education really was.

Many of the students' families struggled to afford the small fee the forum charged for its classes, and some had no money for even one pencil or a few sheets of paper. But the women in charge found a way to make the donated books last longer and to use and reuse the provisions they had. The children shared everything.

Growing the home business projects remained Kamila's favorite part of the job. At the Community Forum headquarters she and her colleagues ran training sessions on the basics of tailoring and quilting. Afterward they would deliver fabric, thread, and needles to women in the Taimani section of Kabul, returning days later to pick up the sweaters and blankets the women had made.

These outings gave Kamila a close-up view of Kabul's poverty. She saw families of seven or even twelve people forced to survive for days on boiled water and a few old potatoes; she knew women who had sold the windows of their homes to feed their children. Some desperate parents she met had sent their little girls and boys, as small as eight and nine, to Pakistan to work. No one knew if they'd ever see them again. She grew even more committed to the

Community Forums' efforts. With all this despair crippling her city, who was she not to do her part?

Soon, Habitat managers asked Kamila and her District 10 colleague Nuria to help with several other forums as well. An experienced teacher and an expert accountant who had finished her studies at Sayed Jamaluddin several years ahead of Kamila, Nuria supported her father and two nephews on her Habitat salary. Each morning, regardless of the cold or the rain, she and Kamila shared the forty-minute walk along the back roads to their center in Taimani, discussing their lessons for the day and ideas for future projects, including a women's center that Mahbooba had suggested they help develop.

Families showed their gratitude for the forum's presence by protecting the women as much as they could. "Tell Nuria and Kamila a new Talib is patrolling the neighborhood; they should be extra careful this morning," the father of one of her students whispered early one morning to a little girl who answered the school's door. He had come running over to warn the women as soon as word of the neighborhood's new minder had reached him. Kamila, Nuria, and three dozen little girls spent the next half hour huddled together on the drafty floor in total silence while the Talib knocked again and again on their door, until at last, hearing nothing, the soldier gave up and moved on. An hour later, once Kamila could convince her heart to stop racing, classes were back up and running.

Everyone, it seemed, had learned how to adapt. And that held for Kamila's house, too. With their sister spending most of her time at the Community Forum, Saaman and Laila had taken over the day-to-day management of the business, naturally assuming the new roles they had been preparing for. Kamila knew the girls could handle the work, but she was delighted to see how easily they took charge of teaching the students and fulfilling all their contracts. Kamila still went to Lycée Myriam most weeks to do the marketing. She also kept for herself the task of visiting Mandawi Bazaar, whose shopkeepers preferred not to place orders in advance but to sift through the dresses Kamila and Rahim brought them and purchase the ones they liked. The downtown bazaar was too far from Khair Khana for her younger sisters to make the trip, Kamila decided, and she refused to let them take the risk of getting caught on their own, far from home. She and Rahim were used to such work and Kamila wanted to keep it that way.

As for Kamila's own protective older sister, things had improved—but only slowly. The weeks immediately following the fight with Malika had been painful, filled with a wordless tension that Kamila found difficult to bear. She missed her sister intensely and craved the advice and encouragement she had relied upon her whole life. She ached with the strange sensation of having lost a loved one she still saw every day.

At last Malika came to Kamila after overhearing her tell the girls about a District 10 embroidery project one evening as the girls were wrapping up their work. For the first time, she seemed resigned to Kamila's decision, though she was still clearly far from being at peace with it.

"Just promise me that you will be discreet and keep your work hidden; don't carry any UN papers or Community Forum forms they could find if they search your bag," she said. She had waited until the younger girls had gone to bed and the two of them were sitting alone in the living room, near Kamila's old sewing station. Kamila detected the lingering note of disappointment in her sister's voice, but concern and love clearly predominated. "And if you have to carry money around the city to pay the women you work with, then take Rahim and get a taxi for goodness' sake. I know that you know what you are doing and that you think all the tailoring work has taught you how to move around the city as if you're nearly invisible, but remember that they only have to catch you once to destroy everything. Your name, your family, your life. Everything. Don't trust anyone other than your colleagues, and never talk about your work in public, even if you think you are the only ones on the street. Be careful all the time: don't ever let your guard down and get comfortable, even for a moment, because that's all it takes for them to arrest you. Okay?"

Kamila wanted to speak but the words failed to come. She nodded her head, over and over, and hugged her sister tightly.

And she prayed she would be able to keep her promise.

9

# *Danger in the*
# *Night Sky*

L oud voices jolted Kamila from her sleep. In a fog she
pulled herself upright and found herself sitting on
the worn vinyl seat of an old Pakistani-made bus.
"We are on the way to Peshawar," she remembered, now
almost fully awake and realizing the bus was no longer
moving. Something must be wrong. . . .

It had been nearly four years since another bus ride
had taken Kamila, with her new diploma in hand, from
Sayed Jamaluddin back to her home in Khair Khana
on the day the Taliban arrived. Kamila thought about it
often—how much had happened since then. She and her
sisters had lived through so much, and she was no longer
a nervous teenager preparing to teach school. Now she
was an entrepreneur and a community leader with the

Women's Community Forum program, and she was on her way to a training session in Peshawar hosted by her international bosses: Samantha, the unrelenting head of UN Habitat who had battled both her own superiors as well as the Taliban to keep the Community Forums running; and Anne, who headed Habitat's programs in Kabul. There would be other foreigners there, too, teaching the Community Forum workers such as herself classes in leadership, management, and business skills. It was an extraordinary opportunity to meet and exchange ideas with talented Habitat women who worked all around Afghanistan. Gathering everyone together in Kabul was impossible given the Taliban's rules, so the women were traveling to Pakistan, where the UN had moved much of its Afghan staff.

Shouts again interrupted Kamila's thoughts.

Through the window of her chadri, Kamila watched as a young Talib yelled questions at Hafiza, her traveling companion and Habitat colleague. Sitting next to Hafiza was Seema, another Community Forum organizer on their team. The soldier, Kamila assumed, must have boarded the bus at the government checkpoint on the edge of Jalalabad while she was dozing.

"Where are you coming from?" the Talib shouted. "Who is your *mahram*? Where is he? Show him to me."

Not only were the women riding to Pakistan without a *mahram* but they were headed to a meeting hosted

by foreigners who worked for the United Nations. Relations between the Taliban and international agencies in
Afghanistan had worsened steadily during the past few
months, and the Amr bil-Maroof was again warning that
Afghan women were not to be employed by foreign aid
organizations. If the angry Talib now questioning Seema
found out about their jobs, there would be big problems
for them all.

Kamila sat quietly, thinking through every possible
scenario that might help them escape the trouble they
were in. Her years of visiting the shops at Lycée Myriam
and Mandawi Bazaar with Rahim had taught her there
was usually a way out of such situations if she could find
the right words. A few weeks earlier a member of the
Vice & Virtue forces bounded into Ali's store just as
Kamila was unwrapping the dresses the shopkeeper had
ordered. Thinking fast on her feet she explained to the
soldier that she was here visiting Ali, a member of her
family. "Thank you very much for checking on us; my
relatives and I appreciate all the hard work that you and
your brothers are doing to keep our city safe. We have
great respect for the Amr bil-Maroof," Kamila had told
the soldier. "I've just come to see my cousin here to try
to sell a few dresses to support my brothers and sisters
at home." The soldier looked almost persuaded but not
quite. "Now surely you have more important work to do
to find real lawbreakers and keep this neighborhood free

of danger and dishonor for all of us, no?" In the end, that seemed to satisfy him and he left her with a warning to "be careful" to speak only with men in her family and to get back home right away, as quickly as possible. "Women should not be out on the streets." Ali remained silent and terrified throughout the exchange, and he asked Kamila afterward how she had dared to speak like that to a Talib. Her answer showed how much she had learned during the years of visits to Lycée Myriam with Rahim: "If I didn't speak to him like a brother," Kamila replied, "he would have been sure we were guilty of doing something wrong, which we were not. You are like my family and we are only trying to work on our family's behalf. If I did not explain myself, there could have been problems for you and me and Rahim." Experiences like this had taught her that many of the men who now worked for the government could be reasoned with as long as one was polite, firm, and respectful.

So far, she now observed, the soldier on the bus was still talking to them, and that was a good sign. If things got quiet, then they were in real danger.

Just then Seema pointed toward a middle-aged man who was sitting a few rows behind her.

"He is our *mahram*," she said, leaning her covered head toward a bearded gentleman who had a kindly, open face that suddenly went tense with fear.

The soldier turned his black-rimmed eyes toward the

middle-aged man and stepped toward his seat, towering over him.

"Is this true?" he demanded.

Kamila and her colleagues were too frightened to look at each other across the aisle of the bus. School examinations had prevented both Rahim and Seema's son, their usual *mahrams* and travel companions, from accompanying them on this trip. Eager to get to their training, the women had decided to go ahead on their own, despite the risks. Rahim had done all he could to help, including purchasing the women's tickets in his own name, though they all knew this would be of little help if they were caught without a male chaperone. The three colleagues had agreed to say, if they were stopped and questioned, that they were family traveling to Peshawar to visit relatives. A few minutes into their journey they had decided on one more precaution and asked their fellow passenger, the man who now sat terrified behind them, to say he was their uncle if the Taliban appeared. This had become standard practice in Kabul, since widows and women without sons or male family members still had to do their shopping, visit their relatives, and take their children to the doctor. The man reassured them with a smile. "No problem, I am here," he had promised.

Now, however, the danger was real and not just theoretical, and this man wanted nothing to do with them. Staring at the Kalashnikov, he deserted them.

"No, it is not true," the man said quietly. "I am not their *mahram*. They are not with me."

The Talib seethed.

"What kind of women are you?" he shouted at Hafiza and Seema. Then he turned and shouted to the driver, "I am taking these women to prison. Now. Call another bus to take the rest of your passengers to the border."

Kamila knew she had to step in.

"My brother, with much respect, I must tell you we are meeting our *mahram* at the border," Kamila began. "My name is Kamila, and my brother Rahim is our *mahram*. He was with us, but I have forgotten my luggage at home and he has gone back to get it for me. He will meet us at the border."

The young soldier was unmoved.

"How can you call yourself a Muslim? What kind of family are you from? This is a disgrace." The barrel of his AK-47 now hovered just inches from Kamila's forehead.

Remembering the paper ticket, Kamila pulled it from her bag, hands shaking.

"Look, you see, here is our proof." She pointed at the slip of paper with Rahim's name written on it. "This ticket is under my brother's name for all of us. He is our *mahram*. He will meet us at the border."

Hafiza and Seema looked on from their seats, motionless.

"We do not wish to violate the law," Kamila went on.

"It is difficult for my aunties and me; we would not choose to travel without our *mahram*. We know the rules, and we respect them. But we cannot go to Pakistan without all our bags and the presents we have in them for the children. How can we go to see our family with nothing? My brother will meet us very soon with our luggage."

The standoff wore on. The soldier asked for her father's name and her family's residence. Then he asked once more about her brother. Twenty minutes passed. Kamila imagined being taken to prison, wondering what she would tell her mother and Malika if she were arrested. This is exactly what her older sister had warned her about when they finally reconciled a few months back, and why she had begged her not to accept the Habitat offer in the first place. Kamila thought of her own harsh words from several months earlier.

"If something does happen to me, I promise I will not come to you to get me out of it. It will be my responsibility."

Now she only hoped her sister would forgive her if she was hauled off to jail here in Jalalabad. Malika was right; it took only a moment for everything to go horribly wrong.

Ignoring her fear and relying on her faith and her experience, she kept on talking, calmly and deferentially. Eventually Kamila realized that she was wearing the soldier down and he was beginning to tire of the situation.

He was still angry but she sensed he was growing restless and was ready to move on to more docile offenders.

The Talib peered at her through the rectangular screen of her burqa. His words came out in a deep growl.

"If you didn't have this ticket I would never allow you to go to Pakistan. Do not travel again without your *mahram*. Next time it will be prison."

He turned around and stepped off the minibus, returning to his post at the checkpoint. Kamila tried not to look in his direction as the driver pulled away and returned to the road once more. The driver, she noticed, looked as pale and shaken as she felt.

For the next hour the women sat stunned and silent, drained of words and energy. The adrenaline that had fueled Kamila's courage was long gone, and she slumped against the window, saying her prayers and thanking Allah for keeping her safe. In a few hours they would be in Peshawar; their training would begin the next day.

❋

When she returned to Kabul, Kamila told her family nothing of what she had encountered on the way to Pakistan. She did not want to worry Malika—or to prove her worst fears right. And she wanted to spare her younger sisters and the students the reminder of what they already knew: the world outside their green gate remained full of danger. Poverty, food shortages, and the merciless drought had drained the life out of everyone in the city, including the Taliban's own soldiers, who patrolled the barren capital in their *shalwar kameez* with little to protect them against the freezing winter. They were struggling to survive almost as much as the citizens they ruled. No one, it seemed, had the energy to fight anymore. Even the Kabul Zoo's lone lion, Marjan, a gift from the Germans in far better times, looked exhausted.

Kamila continued to keep quiet months later when she heard that Wazhma, a friend and Community Forum colleague, had been arrested. It seemed that a neighborhood woman had turned her in to the Amr bil-Maroof for teaching girls in one of the nearby districts; two Taliban had waited for her early in the morning and took her away as soon as she arrived to open the Community Forum school. Though Samantha and Anne, with help from the UN system, were fighting hard to get her out of jail, the Taliban had not yet released her, and rumors of her mistreatment—though unproven—were spreading quickly. Several days into her detention, Wazhma sent word to Kamila through Habitat coworkers who had come to see her in prison that she should stop her work immediately. "Please tell Kamila she should not go to Community Forum anymore," she had said. "Tell her she is too young and has a long life ahead of her; she should not take such risks. I know the forum work is important, but nothing is worth her life." Kamila listened to her friend's warning, but she would not be swayed. She went on working, now even more aware—as if she needed another reminder—of the very real threats she was facing every day. "God will keep me safe," she told herself. "I trust in my faith."

And then all at once a new epidemic hit the city. Thankfully it had nothing whatsoever to do with the Taliban: it was *Titanic* fever.

The epic Hollywood romance had made it to Afghanistan, and like their brethren around the world, young people all over Kabul were swept up in their obsession for the movie. Bootleg VHS tapes of the film were now flying across the city, passed in secret from friend to cousin to neighbor. One acquaintance of Kamila's hid her copy in the bottom of a soup pot that she transported across the Pakistani border; a classmate of Rahim's buried his among tunics rolled up in the bottom of suitcases he carried from Iran. The film could now be found in underground video stores across the capital, and though the pirated cassettes had often been dubbed so many times that entire passages were garbled and had to be skipped over, most people didn't care: they just wanted to hear a few bars of "My Heart Will Go On" and to follow yet again the ill-fated struggle of the star-crossed lovers whose happiness was impossible.

The Taliban's standard arsenal of weapons proved useless against *Titanic*. They scrambled to fight the film's wicked influence, beginning with the "*Titanic* haircut," which they outlawed. They dragged boys they found wearing the floppy-in-the-front style to the barbershop for a full buzz cut. When that strategy proved futile the soldiers went after the barbers themselves, arresting nearly two dozen for giving aspiring Jack Dawsons "the Leo look." Wedding cakes in the form of the famous ocean liner grew popular and were also banned; the Taliban branded them "a violation of Afghanistan's national and Islamic culture."

Still, the craze continued unabated. Entrepreneurs rushed to turn the film's tidal wave of popularity into profit and helped rename the market in the dried bed of the Kabul River, which was now brown and parched from the drought, "Titanic Bazaar." Businessmen plastered the name and image of *Titanic* to anything they could find— storefronts, taxis, shoes, hand lotion, even vegetables and lipsticks. Kamila had seen the movie herself with a group of friends at the home of a girl whose father was close with the local Taliban commander. Afterward she commented to Rahim that it seemed there was nothing in Kabul that remained untouched by the saga of Rose and Jack. "Now that," she said, "is marketing."

Aside from the *Titanic* interlude, life continued on much as it had, interrupted occasionally by the excitement of a letter from Mr. Sidiqi, who wrote from Iran to thank Kamila and the girls for sending money to him and Najeeb through friends and relatives. Mrs. Sidiqi was now living with the girls most of the time, and they watched in sadness as she struggled against her worsening heart condition. They worried continually for her health but Mrs. Sidiqi would have none of it; she refused to stay still and instead busied herself around the house with cooking and cleaning. Her greatest joy now seemed to come from being surrounded by her girls and the young women who arrived at her house each day to work. If Taliban rules and her own fragile constitution conspired to prevent her from being out in the world, at least she could still hear what was happening in her community through the stories of these young ladies.

Meanwhile, orders for the tailoring business continued to come in, and the living room/workroom remained a hive of activity.

One autumn afternoon Saaman and Laila were hard at work on a large batch of wedding dresses, along with a made-to-measure order for a young woman who was marrying a Sidiqi neighbor. The groom was one of the only other people the girls knew who had ties to the international community; he served as a guard at a foreign agency charged with removing the millions of land mines left behind by the Soviets. The Sidiqi girls had heard that his position—and salary—had been invaluable when his brother was jailed for a week in nearby Taimani for the offense of having taught students to draw at a friend's art school. He had only been substitute teaching, but the Taliban had caught him mid-lesson and hauled him off to jail the moment they found art magazines hidden in an office desk drawer.

As they sewed the green and white dresses, the girls listened on their cassette player to the low and lugubrious notes of Ahmad Zahir, still one of Afghanistan's most famous singers though nearly twenty years had passed since his death. The former teacher and *Kabul Times* reporter had been assassinated in 1979 at the age of thirty-three, reportedly on the orders of a communist official who was angered by the popular singer's politics.

Zahir's voice filled the workspace:

*On the one hand, I want to go, to go*
*On the other hand, I don't want to go*
*I don't have the strength*
*What can I do without you*

Just after 5 P.M., Kamila rushed through the gate and the front door. She was now delivering clothes and food to needy Kabulis for another UN agency, the International Organization for Migration, and she was not expected home from her staff meeting for another half-hour. Her cheeks were red and she was out of breath.

"Have you heard the news?" she asked her sisters. "They've killed Massoud."

Laila immediately reached for the radio, and a few

tense minutes later the static of the medium wave gave way to the clear voice of the BBC Persian news service's anchor, who was broadcasting live from London. Mrs. Sidiqi's face grew even more wan as she listened to the foreign voice that was entering her living room from thousands of miles away. The girls gathered around the radio.

"There has been an attack against Ahmad Shah Massoud at his headquarters in Afghanistan's Takhar province," the BBC's Daud Qarizadah said, citing a source close to the Northern Alliance leader. "Massoud has been killed along with several others present." Apparently the men who led the attack had been posing as journalists; they had hidden a bomb in their camera and had been killed themselves in the blast. Mrs. Sidiqi and her daughters knew that Massoud's forces represented the last holdout against the Taliban; for the last few years they were all that had prevented the movement from taking complete control of the country. If Massoud was killed, the Taliban would be rid of their most formidable foe, but the fighting was unlikely to end.

The girls sat stunned and silent. Kamila watched the shock, fear, and despair spread across her mother's face. She refused to believe Massoud was gone; surely he, the Lion of Panjshir, could survive a bomb even if it exploded at close range. He was a veteran of many wars, was he not? He had fought for decades, first against the Russians, then against rival Mujahideen as defense minister, and now against the Taliban. Surely this could not be the end of him?

The next day's reports brought only confusion and more questions. Burhanuddin Rabbani insisted that his former defense minister was still alive, as did Massoud's spokesman, but journalists and officials contradicted them. No one knew what to believe, though everyone suspected the worst.

Sara came to the house at her usual hour and got to work, eager for the distraction from the news. "If the reports are true and he is dead," she said, "things are likely to get worse. The fighting could be even more vicious than it was during the civil war. You girls may yet need to leave the country. I hope I am wrong, but it's possible that things will descend to a level even we have not yet witnessed."

Kamila thought for a moment of her father and how badly she missed his wisdom and reassurance. But she refused to give up hope.

The next twenty-four hours saw little work done in the Sidiqi household, and then came more disastrous news: two airliners had flown into the World Trade Center in New York City and thousands were believed dead, though the rescue effort was just beginning. Another plane had crashed into the Pentagon near the American capital of Washington, D.C., and a fourth had failed to reach its target, which many guessed was the White House. The world was off its hinge.

To his mother's relief, Rahim came home early from school, saying that no one was paying any attention to classes; they were only talking about the news of the past two days and wondering what would happen next. Most everyone in the capital had immediately assumed that Osama bin Laden, the wealthy Saudi who had been living in the country as the Taliban's guest, was involved in the attack against America. Years earlier the United States had bombed suspected bin Laden training camps in eastern Afghanistan in retaliation for attacks on two American embassies in Africa. Washington had demanded that the Taliban turn bin Laden over to U.S. authorities, but the regime refused to revoke its hospitality. Their guest should be tried in Afghanistan for whatever offenses the Americans were accusing him of. Hostilities between the United States and the Taliban had worsened ever since. Now the Americans claimed they had evidence that bin Laden was behind the bloody 9/11 plot and they again insisted that the Taliban turn him over. Once more, the Taliban leaders refused.

The Sidiqis, like most Afghans, had only a vague sense of who the Taliban's "Arabs" were. The men were widely thought to be fighters from Saudi Arabia, Egypt, Chechnya, Yemen, Somalia, and elsewhere who had come to join the Taliban's cause at the behest of bin Laden. When the Taliban movement first began, its leaders had presented themselves not as enemies of the West but as humble purifiers of their own country, committed to restoring a desperately needed peace. But as the years passed and international recognition eluded them, the leadership adopted increasingly angry rhetoric against the United States and moved ever closer to bin Laden and his organization, which went by the name Al Qaeda, or "the base" in Arabic. This relationship only deepened after the United Nations imposed military and economic sanctions on the Taliban, leaving the regime even more isolated than it had previously been when only three countries in the world had recognized its legitimacy.

Al Qaeda's fighters were thought to be responsible for the attack on Massoud, according to news reports that at last confirmed irrefutably the Northern Alliance leader's death. And now they were rumored to be behind the strikes against the United States.

Mrs. Sidiqi and her girls knew only what they had heard on the BBC and the classroom rumors that Rahim came home with. But that was enough to make it clear that Afghanistan was at the center of the past week's horrors and would certainly be the target of whatever retaliation would follow. The U.S. government was already threatening to strike back if the Taliban did not hand over bin Laden. And no one in Kabul had any reason to think that they would. For years Afghanistan had lived as a pariah nation, utterly forgotten by the rest of world. Now no one on the radio talked of anyplace else.

And so the waiting game began. What little economic life had managed to survive in the capital came to a sudden halt as the citizens of Kabul held their collective breath. Everyone knew their destiny now lay in the hands of men in Kandahar, Washington, London, and other unknown and faraway capitals. Gossip spread like wildfire, as it always did in Kabul, passed along by families, neighbors, and shopkeepers. The city's most seasoned observers believed a military attack by the Americans against the Taliban government was imminent—and unavoidable. The girls heard that the UN was evacuating its staff in anticipation of war; they wondered what the internationals knew that they didn't.

Brace yourself.

Stay indoors.

And pray.

That was all that was left for most Kabulis.

Those who could, however, were determined to get out. The smattering of families still living on Kamila's street were packing up their few belongings and evacuating the city. They would head for Pakistan if they could get that far, or the Afghan countryside if they couldn't, and they urged Mrs. Sidiqi to do the same. This was no place for her and her children; surely the Americans' bombs would soon rain down upon all of them. You had better get out of here as soon as you can, their neighbors warned. Khair Khana is teeming with targets: the airport, the fuel depot,

Taliban artillery units. All of them were located within just two or three miles of Kamila's house. Even Sara urged Mrs. Sidiqi and the girls to leave their home; she herself was taking her children to live in another part of Khair Khana, a few miles farther from the airport. The risk of staying put was just too high, she said. What happens if the Americans miss?

As the economy withered in the weeks following the attacks of September 11, the price for passage out of the capital skyrocketed. Trucks, buses, and taxis overflowed with families seeking safer places, with fares reaching as high as five hundred dollars. People rushed to money changers by the Kabul River to exchange savings they held in Pakistani and Iranian currencies into afghani so they could buy food and other supplies. But the rates moved against them by the day. The city's savvy traders were betting American dollars would soon be entering the country once the Taliban government fell. After the war.

Mrs. Sidiqi heard the stories and watched her neighbor's preparations. But she remained convinced that her family was best off staying exactly where it was. There would be no fleeing for them. If something happened to her or her girls while they were in their own home, that was one thing, and she would leave it to God's will. But she would not have her precious daughters made vulnerable to the kidnappers, murderers, and bandits who awaited them once they left the security of their own courtyard. They were better off here, together, off the streets and far from the bedlam outside.

※

Four weeks after Massoud's death and the attacks of September 11, the barrage began. Just after the girls finished dinner one evening, missiles whizzed across the night sky and the boom of explosions was heard around Kabul. Sitting in her bedroom, Kamila felt the windows shudder and the floors shake while Nasrin and Laila ran to look for their mother and their older sisters, crying out in terror as they ran down the long hall that connected the living room to the family's sleeping chambers. The house turned black in an instant as the Taliban cut the city's power supply in hopes of throwing off the enemy planes that roared overhead. They heard the sharp rat-tat-tat sound of the Taliban's lumbering antiaircraft guns chasing the foreigners' jets around the city in their black trucks, attempting in vain to hit the elusive American aircraft soaring unfazed up above.

And finally, silence.

Kamila sat with fourteen-year-old Nasrin for another hour, cuddling her in her lap. "It's all over," she whispered. "Everyone's okay. See? We're all here, just fine." She patted her little sister on the back and hoped the girl wouldn't notice how uncontrollably her own hands were trembling.

Dawn arrived and a new day began as if it were any

other. Shops and offices opened and the clear autumn sun shone cheerily. But terror and uncertainty had settled over the capital. Panicked families were clamoring to leave, struggling to find a way out before dark, when the bombs were likely to start pummeling the city once more. Rahim, returning from the market, reported that Khair Khana's streets looked like a graveyard. Finding food was no problem, he said; he had the shops to himself since everyone else was busy planning their escape.

The fighting ground on for one week and then another, with an occasional break on Friday, the Muslim holy day. The family grew accustomed to early dinners followed by a tense, candlelit evening in the windowless bedroom waiting for the night air to fill with the boom of jets and the thud of explosions. Like many Kabulis, Rahim and the girls came to know the distinct sounds that each warplane made. They were fluent in the differences among B-52s, B-2s, F-14s, and AC-130s. They learned about "cluster bombs" and "smart bombs." And they were now sorrowfully familiar with the stench of sour smoke that steamed up from the ground in the wake of each night's air raids.

Khair Khana reeled under the relentless pounding of the American air blitz, which sometimes began long before nightfall. Sara Jan was right, Kamila thought. No one is safe here. Bombs dropped from the sky sometimes landed so close that Kamila was shocked to open her eyes and see that her house was still standing. She now felt certain that she would not survive. American planes targeted neighborhood Taliban sites night after night, leaving behind deafening explosions and cratered streets. One afternoon a week after the aerial assault began, a bomb demolished two homes in another part of Khair Khana and killed seven people inside. The intended target appeared to be a military garrison a few miles away. Word of the deaths spread swiftly among the few families who were still living in Khair Khana, and with it came even more fear.

"Stay in your houses!" Taliban soldiers shouted on the nights they patrolled the streets of Khair Khana. The government had blocked all of Kabul's main roads and instituted an even earlier curfew now that the Americans had attacked. They needn't bother, Kamila thought, hearing the soldiers' warnings pierce the silence on the street outside her gate. *The whole city is under fire. Where are we going to go?*

Each evening Kamila and Saaman tuned the battery-powered radio to the BBC's broadcast to hear the latest on the fighting. The news anchors in London now regularly raised the possibility that the Taliban regime would be replaced; the men from Kandahar, they reported, would eventually be forced to retreat before the overwhelming air strikes of the Americans, who were deploying the twenty-first century's most powerful technology against their cars, trucks, bunkers, barracks, radio stations, airports, weapons depots, and trenches. None of the girls dared to discuss out loud what would happen if or when the Taliban government gave up, though the voices on the medium-wave suggested that Zahir Shah, the former king, might possibly return to rule the country. Kamila and her sisters had no way of knowing how much longer the war would go on. Or whether they would live through it.

Kamila depended on her faith to help her endure the terrifying offensive and stay strong for her younger sisters. She prayed for her country, which had known nothing but war and bloodshed for her entire life. Despite the fighting that now engulfed her home and her city, she wanted to believe that whatever came next, the future would be brighter.

Peace and a chance to pursue our dreams, Kamila thought to herself one night when it seemed there would be no end to the blasts that rocked the earth beneath her. That's all we can dare to hope for.

For now, she thought, it would have to be enough.

# *Kabul Jan, Kaweyan, and Kamila's Faith in Good Fortune*

On November 13, 2001, the Taliban abandoned Kabul.

Radio Sharia once again became Radio Afghanistan. And Farhad Darya's voice rang out in his song "Kabul Jan" ("Beloved Kabul"), this time in the open, for everyone to enjoy, with no Amr bil-Maroof to fear:

*Let me sing the hymn of the Afghan nation*
*Let me go to Hindukush and recite the Holy Q'uran*
*Let me sing to my homeless wandering people*
*From Iran all the way down to Pakistan*

Northern Alliance soldiers in their crisp camouflage uniforms spread out across the capital, riding up and down city streets and shouting that the Taliban had gone. On Khair Khana's main road, Indian songs blared from shops and stalls. Cars honked their horns. Men shaved their beards on the streets. Children brought out their soccer balls. The city relaxed—and celebrated publicly—for the first time in five years.

To most of Kabul's women, however, the party outside felt decidedly premature. Mrs. Sidiqi was so worried about the chaos in the streets and the sudden change of government that she sent all five of her girls into a crawlspace under the stairs that led up to Dr. Maryam's office and ordered them to stay there until she judged it safe for them to come out. "Who knows what will happen?" she said to the girls as she shooed them into the little windowless storage area. Who knew if marauding men would wander into their home now that the Taliban had fled? "Wait here until tomorrow; then we'll know better." All night long the girls listened to the muffled sound of street celebrations from their bunker.

For days afterward, female visitors arrived at the green gate still wearing their chadri. Kamila agreed with her friends that it was wise to wait before shedding the veil they had gotten so used to over the past five years. No need to rush. If things really had changed, there would be plenty of time to adjust to the new order and embrace their hard-won liberties.

❋

By the time I met Kamila, in December 2005, the first stage of the war had long since passed, and so had the euphoria that greeted the American invasion and the retreat of the Taliban. Many Afghans I interviewed wondered why things weren't getting better. They pilloried the free-spending foreigners for their wasteful ways: the big cars that hogged the torn-up roads, the expensive fortified compounds, the well-intended development projects—and their well-paid staffs—which left little behind once they ended. The more time I spent in Kabul the more I saw what they saw and the more I understood their frustration. I also wondered if this latest international foray into Afghan nation-building would end well for anyone.

Perhaps that's why the first thing I noticed about Kamila—other than her ebullient youth—was her optimism. Her faith upended my own mounting despair. She spoke about her country's promise with conviction and hope. Not a trace of skepticism or cynicism. "When the international community returned to Afghanistan in 2001," she told me, "it was as though they suddenly remembered our country just as quickly as they had forgotten it, after they abandoned us once the Soviets left." And Kamila welcomed the world back with open arms. "This is a golden chance for Afghanistan," she said. An opportunity to help her fellow Afghans rebuild what war had destroyed: the roads, the economy, the country's educational system—all the vital infrastructure that had collapsed—and to give her generation and the next one the first chance they had ever had to live in peace. For the past four years Kamila had been doing her part, working with the foreigners on behalf of her countrymen, first with the United Nations and then with the global aid organization Mercy Corps. Women like her who had experience with the international community were in short supply and high demand.

Kamila's work after the American invasion and the fall of the Taliban focused on women and business. Soon after the Taliban troops pulled out of Kabul she left the International Organization for Migration to set up and staff a Mercy Corps women's center in Kabul that offered literacy classes and vocational courses. She trained women in microfinance, teaching them how to use small loans to grow vegetables or make soap and candles, and how to sell these products once they were ready for market. The key was to help women help themselves so that they could support their families long after the foreigners left.

As she got better at her work, Kamila began to train other business teachers, and she traveled around the country leading courses in entrepreneurship. She could connect to uneducated and illiterate Afghans much better than the highly paid foreign consultants could, and she was adept at bridging the gap between her international bosses and the people they had come to Afghanistan to help. Mercy Corps colleagues, including Anita, who first recruited her to the organization, and Shireen, a former journalist who had worked for AT&T, helped Kamila to fill any gaps in her knowledge.

But as much as she enjoyed her work for the big global organizations, Kamila never lost the entrepreneurship bug herself. While working at Mercy Corps she started a construction business. The company thrived for a while, but it was hard to find the capital to keep it going, and competition was fierce. So she closed it down and began looking for other opportunities.

Kamila's colleagues became part of her family just as they had when she ran her tailoring business. Only this time it was members of the international community who passed through the green gate, not determined young women looking for work. It was nothing unusual to have coworkers from France or Canada show up for dinner at the Sidiqi home, and one foreign friend even moved in with the Sidiqi clan so they could help her improve her Dari language skills. Ruxandra, a consultant with the International Labour Organization, whose work and research focused on women and business, was a regular visitor. Kamila's parents were amazed by the salaries the foreigners were paying. Young women like Kamila who had worked for the UN and NGOs under the Taliban now earned nearly as much in one week as they had in a year. The money Kamila brought home funded the university education of her brothers and sisters as well as the upkeep of the house in Khair Khana, where most of the siblings now lived.

As always, Malika tried to encourage her younger sister, offering advice when asked but otherwise staying out of her way. She marveled at how quickly her sister adapted to the end of the Taliban and the arrival of the foreigners, and watched in pride as Kamila unleashed all the ambition and talent she had stored up in the Taliban days now that Afghanistan had rejoined the rest of the world.

In January 2005, the Thunderbird School of Global Management, located in the United States, in Arizona, accepted Kamila to a two-week MBA program for Afghan businesswomen; already she had been invited to join Bpeace, a New York nonprofit that ran a mentoring program for high-potential entrepreneurs. And then one day in October the phone rang and Kamila learned that Condoleezza Rice, the American secretary of state, had invited her—the dressmaker from Kabul who had started a construction company—to Washington, D.C. Just days later she found herself speaking into a shiny microphone and peering out at a sea of tables set with linen tablecloths and glimmering crystal and around which sat Very Important People—members of Congress, businessmen, diplomats, and the secretary of state herself—who were there to hear her story:

"I am Kamila Sidiqi," she began. "I am a business

owner from Afghanistan. . . ." She told them how she started her first venture from the living room of her home in Khair Khana, and how today—with the help of Thunderbird, Mercy Corps, and U.S. government funding—she had trained more than nine hundred of her countrymen and women so that they, too, would have the skills to build and grow their own businesses. She spoke about how business and education transformed women's lives, and how this change had led to another extraordinary development: women in Afghanistan taking part in the political process. "This partnership between America and my country, it's a good and helpful beginning. Together, I believe that we can and will make even more progress in building a more stable and successful Afghanistan."

❋

I met Kamila for a cup of tea about a month after her Washington speech in the Mercy Corps' Kabul offices. It was a somewhat cheerless winter afternoon and she was at a crossroads. After attending a business development services training in Italy sponsored by Mercy Corps, she had decided to abandon her work for international agencies and begin her own business—again. She was about to turn down a good job that offered her stability and some security, and she had no doubts about her decision.

"If I go to work with some international agency they

will give me a very high salary but it really only benefits just my family and me," she told me. "It doesn't create jobs for other people, like we did during the Taliban. On the other hand, if I start my own private company, I can train a lot of people, and those people will go out and start their own businesses. And then maybe they will inspire even more people to do the same thing, and so on. I know this business could make a big difference for this country."

It was her beloved brother Najeeb who came up with the name for Kamila's new enterprise. Her dressmaking business had supported him during the Taliban years, and the word that he found to capture his sister's energy and aspiration was *Kaweyan*, after an eastern Iranian dynasty that was known for its glory and good fortune. Najeeb confidently predicted that his sister would have the same lasting success.

At this time, though, Kamila was Kaweyan's sole employee, and its only assets were a silver Dell laptop—courtesy of Mercy Corps—and the clear, passionate vision of its young founder.

"Once I have launched this business," she said, "I will start training people—both men and women—and create mobile teams that can travel to different provinces all over Afghanistan and maybe even Pakistan and India. Kaweyan will teach people to develop their ideas and write a business plan, to make a budget and do profit-and-loss analysis. Later on we can work with private companies on marketing and business ideas, because Afghanistan needs business if it is going to keep growing once the foreigners leave. And I want to work with students, too, just as we did with the tailoring business: Kaweyan could give part-time work to university interns so they can write business plans for all different kinds of companies around the country. We don't have enough jobs for everyone in Afghanistan, and this way we'll create opportunities for young people as well as entrepreneurs."

Women, of course, would be a particular focus of Kaweyan. After so many years of war, women's entrepreneurship was about far more than business.

"Money is power for women," Kamila said. "If women have their own income to bring to the family, they can contribute and make decisions. Their brothers, their husbands, and their entire families will have respect for them. I've seen this again and again. It's so important in Afghanistan because women have always had to ask for money from men. If we can give them some training, and an ability to earn a good salary, then we can change their lives and help their families."

She paused for a moment to make sure I was following, then continued. "I was lucky. My father was a very educated man and he made certain that all nine of his daughters studied and learned. But there are families everywhere who have six or seven children and they can only pay for the boys to go to school; they don't have enough money for girls to go. So if we can train a woman who never had the chance to study, and she can start her own business, it will be good for the whole family as well as for the community. Her work will create jobs for other people and pay for both her boys and her girls to be educated. For the future of Afghanistan we must provide good education for our children—for the next generation. That's why business matters. And that's why I started Kaweyan."

Over the years that I spent visiting with Kamila, she and I kept up a running joke that we both needed to get married soon, if only to stop our families from asking us when we would. I thought it funny that though the worlds we came from could not be any more different, we shared a similar set of pressures from relatives who, though proud of our work, were eager to see us find good husbands and "finally settle down."

And by the time 2008 finished, both of us had—happily. Kamila's groom was a cousin who had studied engineering in Moscow and now lived in London. Though she had no doubt she wanted to marry him, she insisted during their long months of courtship by phone and email that he understand and accept how committed she was to her business and to Afghanistan. With the delight of a new bride she showed me a wallet-size photo of him that she carried with her. He has a movie-star smile and, she says, a generous heart paired with a powerful intellect.

Their 2007 wedding was a glorious, two-day, 650-guest Afghan affair with pounding music and endless meals. Kamila shone in an intricately beaded, long-sleeved white gown. (Saaman's earlier prediction turned out to be true: Kamila no longer had time to sew anything herself and found both of her dresses at a fashionable downtown store.) Looking as glamorous as a film star, she posed with her handsome new husband for picture after picture. Mr. Sidiqi, always noticeable for his impeccable military posture, beams in the photos, looking every inch the proud patriarch.

A year later Kamila gave birth to a baby boy, Naweyan. She takes him to Kaweyan's second-story office nearly every morning—sometimes to her out-of-town trainings, too—and jokes that he is the firm's youngest employee. He sleeps through most of her meetings, only occasionally waking up to interrupt his mother's discussions with cries of hunger. When he gets very fussy one of Kamila's eight sisters comes by the office to take him home for the afternoon. I confess that, as I watched the infant's handoff among the sisters, it sometimes seemed easier to be a working mom in Kabul than in Washington.

On my last reporting trip to Afghanistan, in October 2009, I met Kamila's older brother, Najeeb. He had spent most of the Taliban years in Iran, working odd jobs, before returning to university study and a prestigious public service position in Kabul. We had arranged to meet at the Kabul Inn, a quiet hotel with a modest dining room that looked onto a courtyard filled with flowering shrubs that shook in the winter wind. Indian music videos loudly played on a TV set in the corner near an abandoned buffet table. An hour had passed since our scheduled meeting time, and I began to worry. Perhaps he had decided not to come; perhaps he worried that telling his sister's—and his family's—story was unwise in the current political climate. But finally he rushed through the door and apologized for his lateness. Roads were blocked all across downtown Kabul in hopes of thwarting suicide attacks around the upcoming presidential runoff elections; it had taken him ninety minutes to go only a few kilometers.

I waited nervously for him to begin.

"Gayle Jan," he said, "I wanted to meet you because I wanted to thank you. I always hoped that someone would come from a foreign country and tell my sister's story. She was so brave at such a difficult time, and she did so much for all of us—not just my own family but so many other families in Khair Khana and around Kabul. And she is the reason that all of us got educated. I wanted you to know how glad I am that her story will finally be told. And to thank you for coming here."

For the first time since arriving bleary-eyed in Afghanistan that sunny December morning—for the first time ever on a reporting trip, I admit—my eyes teared. And I realized that Kamila's brother understood better than I did why, at this moment, telling his sister's story matters so much. Brave young women complete heroic acts every day, with no one bearing witness. This was a chance to even the ledger, to share one small story that made the difference between starvation and survival for the families whose lives it changed. I wanted to pull the curtain back for readers on a place foreigners know more for its rocket attacks and roadside bombs than its countless quiet feats of courage. And to introduce them to the young women like Kamila Sidiqi who will go on. No matter what.

# Where They Are Today

**Sara** continues to work for the betterment of her family. Her two sons are enrolled in university, which makes her very proud, and her work allows her to afford a home for her family so she no longer has to be a financial burden on her in-laws. Today she and her children are living on their own in the capital. Sara continues to work as a seamstress while also serving as a cook and house manager.

**Mahnaz** went on to achieve her dream of becoming an educator. Though it was difficult for her to resume her studies after the five-and-a-half-year ban on girls' education, she persevered, taking the university entrance exam and landing a position as a young professor at one of Kabul's leading institutions of higher education. For two years after the Taliban departed, she continued to wear the chadri, finding it difficult to adjust to the change of being out on the street in a mere headscarf. Her sister, who also sewed with Kamila and her sisters, resumed her studies alongside Mahnaz and went on to become a doctor, just as she had always hoped.

In 1998, after nearly two years of Taliban rule, **Dr. Maryam** decided to move her family to Helmand province in southern Afghanistan, right next door to the seat of the Taliban. Few women doctors worked in that region at the time, and she was both adored and respected by her community for the services she provided. Taliban officials were also grateful for her work and for her willingness to leave Kabul, and they did nothing to interfere with the treatment of her patients. Many of them, in fact, brought their wives and daughters to her. Some of the women in Helmand whom Dr. Maryam hired and trained during the Taliban years went on to become nurses and midwives themselves, teaching others in their communities about the importance of protecting women's health. Dr. Maryam continues to work as a pediatrician and encourages her talented young daughters, who are now at the top of their own classes, to consider a career in medicine.

**Rahela**, Kamila's impressive cousin who helped to lead the UN Habitat efforts during the Taliban years, is now a senior government official. She is currently leading an effort to strengthen the country's civil service and, in between managing a demanding career and a family of young children, is also helping to organize and deliver microloans to women in need in two provinces of Afghanistan. In the coming years she hopes to grow the program, which is funded by donations from local women leaders in the community.

Most of the women involved in the Women's Community Forums programs went on to become leaders in their fields. Many are serving in government, a number are educators, some are running their own community organizations, and others have succeeded in business. All credit the Community Forum program with helping them to discover their leadership potential and to prove to themselves that they did indeed have the ability to make a difference.

As for the UN Habitat Community Forum program itself, it became a role model for the new government's plan to develop rural Afghanistan. The National Solidarity Program built upon the Community Forum's democratic and ground-up model using new Community Development Councils to empower citizens to decide on local development priorities for themselves.

**Ali and his brothers** are still in Kabul. Though they no longer have their own stores, they continue to support their families and each other. And they refuse to take credit for the good work they did during those difficult years when Kabul's economy collapsed. Only one of the brothers has seen Roya, their former client, since the Taliban left and the government changed. This accidental meeting came in 2004 when Kamila found herself in a taxi with a driver she recognized. He did not recognize her, since he had never before seen her face, so Kamila/Roya introduced herself to Hamid. He marveled at meeting his longtime client and sent his best wishes to her family. Kamila returned his kindness and added that she and her family remained very grateful for all the support he and his brothers had offered them during the Taliban years.

As for Kamila's sisters, they, too, have forged their own paths, supporting one another and their own families. **Saaman**, who never forgot the joy and beauty of the novels and poetry that had so lifted her spirits through the difficult years, went on to make her family proud by completing her university studies and taking a degree in literature. **Laila** also successfully completed her university courses. **Malika** is now among the busiest women in Kabul, managing all at once to help her husband, raise four healthy children, work with Kamila at Kaweyan, and complete her long-deferred university degree. After sifting through years of memories to tell me about the women she worked with and sewed for during the Taliban years, she remembered the satisfaction she found in her tailoring work and was inspired to resume her dressmaking. She is now once again creating suits, dresses, and jackets for private clients, with help and support from Saaman.

As for **Mr. and Mrs. Sidiqi**, they continue to live in the north, enjoying the beauty of Parwan and relishing visits from their eleven children and dozens of grandchildren. Mr. Sidiqi remains among the most ardent and articulate supporters of girls' education I've ever met. As he often says, "It is much better to earn a living with a pen than with power," and it is a never-ending source of pride to him that all his daughters have been educated. The youngest of his nine girls is now finishing her college studies in computer sciences.

**Kamila's brothers** also succeeded in their studies. Both men completed university degrees that were funded by their sister's work, and each expresses tremendous gratitude for his sister's encouragement and support— emotional as well as financial—over the past fifteen years.

As Najeeb told me, "Besides being my sister, Kamila is my friend and a leader in our family."

Afghanistan's future remained very much on the minds of Kamila and her family as they finally began to look ahead in our conversations, after so many months of looking back. Their belief in their country's potential is powerful, unflagging, and often, I found, beguilingly contagious. Kamila continues to dream big, working to grow Kaweyan and to become one of the nation's leading entrepreneurs. Each day she defies the many setbacks that face her and others who are trying to make a difference in Afghanistan: escalating violence, rising corruption, and an increasingly anxious international community whose work is now regularly aborted by security lockdowns and intensifying threats to its safety.

Women I have met want nothing more than peace. But they fear that the world is growing eager to reach a deal in which their rights will be part of the price of security. And they worry their country's problems will be balanced on their backs once more. Neither they nor the men I have interviewed in the past two years believe that an abandoned Afghanistan will remain an isolated problem for long.

With grace and dignity the individuals to whom this story belongs push forward each day. They believe, as they always have, that something better is possible.

I, for one, hope they are right.

After years of working with Afghan women as an entrepreneur and community leader, Kamila was invited to Washington, D.C., to address the U.S. Global Leadership Campaign's 10th Anniversary Gala Dinner. *(U.S. Global Leadership Campaign)*

# Acknowledgments

This story grew out of reporting I began in 2005 during my first and second year of MBA study following nearly ten years in daily news. I believed then and believe even more strongly now that the stories of women entrepreneurs, particularly in countries fighting to recover from conflict, are worth telling. Not only are these courageous women working each day to strengthen their families and grow their economies; they are also serving as role models for the next generation of young men and women who can see firsthand and for themselves the power of businesswomen to make a difference.

I want to thank all the individuals interviewed who made this story possible. This begins with Kamila and her large and welcoming family, who crammed interviews into their busy days packed with work and children. They opened up their homes and shared their histories, and I am deeply grateful for their immense generosity and their unwavering hospitality amid even the most challenging circumstances. During the years of research and reporting on the story of Kamila and her sisters, I learned just how many young women went to work each day on behalf of their families during the Taliban years despite being shut out of classrooms and offices. The efforts of these un-heralded heroines who joined NGOs, staffed home busi-nesses, and taught classes at hospitals and homes around the city meant the difference between survival and star-vation for many families. It is a privilege to me to share their stories of perseverance and persistence in the face of constantly evolving obstacles.

I offer my humble thanks to the young women who worked with Kamila. For many of them, I was the first foreigner they had ever met and ours was the first inter-view they had ever done. Despite their initial nervousness, they shared their experiences and their impressions from those bleak years whose memories haunt them more than a decade later. For them, Kamila's house was a refuge and a haven from their problems as much as it was their place of work. I have striven to stay true to both the facts and the spirit of these young women's stories: they were bread-winners and valued employees at a time when families had no place else to turn.

ACKNOWLEDGMENTS

To the shopkeepers who worked with Kamila I owe thanks for not only their stories but their hospitality. They graciously sat for hours of interviews both at their offices and in their sitting rooms not because they found their own story at all compelling or welcomed the attention, but because they were glad to help the visiting foreigner who had so many questions about all the work they did so many years ago. Their lives have long moved past that period, but their humility, character, and courage have not dimmed with time.

To the women involved in the Community Forum programs, I want to offer my appreciation for sharing so many details about how and why the program proved so powerful. In listening to a formidable roster of forum alumni discuss their work, which served as a source of hope at so difficult a time, I saw just how much this Herculean effort to keep women working during the Taliban years meant to so many. Their sterling record of grassroots, community-owned organization, mobilization, and leadership is among the most significant success stories I have seen during years of tracking what works—and what doesn't—when it comes to development projects.

Heartfelt thanks to the dozens of international aid workers who lived in Afghanistan during the Mujahideen and Taliban years and who patiently shared their varied impressions of the period during late-night Skype calls with imperfect connections given our far-flung locales. This includes Samantha Reynolds, a leader of vision and conviction, who fought relentlessly for jobs for women even when many other international agencies had largely abandoned the idea. Her staff still remembers her as among the best and most praiseworthy managers they have ever had. Reynolds's boss at the time, Jolyon Leslie, also offered a powerful assembly of sharp insights, and I am grateful for both his time and his perspective. Sincere thanks also to Anne Lancelot and Teresa Poppelwell, Samantha's colleagues at UN Habitat. Lancelot's book, *Burqas, foulards et minijupes: Paroles d'Afghanes*, is a must for any reader seeking to better understand the lives of women during the Taliban period. Thanks also to Anders Fänge, Charles MacFadden, Barbara Rodey, Pippa Bradford, Patricia McPhillips, Henning Scharpff, Norah Niland, and Anita Anastacio, all of whom took hours from their busy days to talk with me about their experiences managing aid and relief programs under the Taliban government.

A number of talented journalists and researchers also generously offered their thoughts, clips, and photos. Thanks to all of them, including Daud Qarizadah, Gretchen Peters, Niazai Sangar, and Amir Shah.

Nancy Dupree and her extraordinary staff at the Afghanistan Center Kabul University (ACKU) offered inordinate amounts of help when I was researching primary documents from the Mujahideen and Taliban years.

ACKU offers documents that cannot be found elsewhere and has a knowledgeable and diligent staff whose assistance is invaluable. Research days spent sifting through archival material at a computer on the library's second floor were productive beyond imagining. Nancy's unrelenting vigor and dedication to doing good offers an example I hope to be worthy of one day.

Reporting from Kabul is a team effort. I want to thank my colleague Mohamad for his journalistic dedication and his commitment to excellence. This work would have been impossible without his translation assistance, his ability to navigate any logistical challenge, and his ready deployment of finely honed problem-solving skills. Thanks also to his wonderful family for their hospitality and their friendship. And to Saibrullah, a driver with a great sense of humor and an uncanny ability to remember any address, even years later.

The *Financial Times'* International Entrepreneurship editor James Pickford was the first person to buy these stories, first from Rwanda and later from Afghanistan, and for this start I am most thankful. My appreciation also to Anne Bagamery at the *International Herald Tribune* and Amelia Newcomb at the *Christian Science Monitor*. Both of these terrific editors helped me bring to their readers stories from Afghanistan that were even stronger and more compelling for their input. And to Tina Brown, Jane Spencer, and Dana Goldstein of the *Daily Beast*, my sincere thanks for giving voice to powerful stories that might otherwise never have been told.

Thanks also to Professor Geoffrey Jones and Regina Abrami at Harvard Business School. They, along with Janet Hanson of 85 Broads and Alex Shkolnikov of CIPE, believed in the potential and the power of these stories when few others did. For their faith I am most grateful.

And to Mohamed El-Erian and my generous PIMCO bosses and colleagues, thank you for providing the support and the time to complete this work.

A slew of extraordinary women supported this research on women's entrepreneurship with their constant encouragement and their own examples of hard-driving excellence. This includes the World Bank's Amanda Ellis, a sometime collaborator and constant inspiration, and 10,000 Women's Dina Powell, an indefatigable advocate in promoting the potential of women as well as a role model for anyone who wants to see just how much is possible when ideas are transformed into action. Thanks also to Alyse Nelson at Vital Voices, whose leadership, commitment, and support are sincerely appreciated. And to Isobel Coleman at the Council on Foreign Relations, whose writing and research have helped to lead the way.

Since I started writing about this topic five years ago, many readers have asked how they can help. To answer this question, I have created a list of just a few of the many organizations that support women in Afghanistan in the pages which follow. You can find out more about them and link to their websites at www.gaylelemmon.com.

Elyse Cheney and Nicole Steen saw the potential in this project at the outset and offered their invaluable support and guidance throughout the journey that led to this book. I don't imagine any writer could ask for a better advocate than Elyse, and I am thankful for her energy and editorial hand. Lisa Sharkey at HarperCollins believed in the idea and introduced me to my editor, thought partner, and friend Julia Cheiffetz at Harper. She and Katie Salisbury have shepherded this book through all the twists and turns of the process, and I am deeply grateful for their relentlessness and their dedication. I am equally grateful to the indefatigable Heather Drucker, who frought hard for this story. Thanks also to Harper's Jonathan Burnham for his commitment to the project. And to Yuli Masinovsky, my thanks for helping all of this get started so long ago. Heartfelt thanks also to Annik LaFarge, a keen judge of character, a generous friend, and a valued voice I could not admire more.

A final thanks to my husband. Without his steady support and unswerving faith in this project, nothing would be the same and far less would be possible.

# Select Bibliography

Adamec, L. W., and F. A. Clements (2003). *Conflict in Afghanistan: An Encyclopedia*. Santa Barbara, CA: ABC-CLIO.

Afghanistan Department for Preservation of Virtue and Prevention of Vice (1997). Reply to TDH letter dated July 27, 1997.

Afghanistan Women's Council (1999). December 1999 Report. Peshawar: Afghanistan Women's Council.

Agency Coordinating Body for Afghan Relief (1996). Edicts Issued by the Taliban Government in Afghanistan. Kabul: Agency Coordinating Body for Afghan Relief.

—— (1996). Kabul After the Taliban Takeover. Peshawar: Agency Coordinating Body for Afghan Relief.

—— (1996). Memo on Shariate (Islamic law) Based Regulations for Hospitals and Private Clinics. Kabul: Agency Coordinating Body for Afghan Relief.

—— (1997). Changing the Name of Government to Emirate: Decree of the Islamic Emirate of Afghanistan. Kandahar and Kabul: Agency Coordinating Body for Afghan Relief.

—— (1998). Ministers and Deputy Ministers of the Islamic Emirate of Afghanistan. Kabul: Agency Coordinating Body for Afghan Relief.

—— (2000). Impact of Edict on Afghan Women Employment on Health Sector. Kabul: Agency Coordinating Body for Afghan Relief.

—— (2001). Memo on the Islamic Emirate of Afghanistan Decree in Relation to the Stay of Foreign Nationals on the Territory of Islamic Emirate of Afghanistan. Peshawar: Agency Coordinating Body for Afghan Relief.

Amnesty International (1999). *Women in Afghanistan: Pawns in Men's Power Struggles.*

Bernard, M., et al. (1996). Socio-economic Household Survey Kabul: December 1996. Kabul: Action contre la Faim.

Crews, R. D., and A. Tarzi, eds. (2008). *The Taliban and the Crisis of Afghanistan.* Cambridge, MA: Harvard University Press.

Donini, A., N. Niland, and K. Wermester, eds. (2004). *Nation-Building Unraveled? Aid, Peace and Justice in Afghanistan.* Bloomfield, CT: Kumarian.

Dorronsoro, G. (2005). *Revolution Unending: Afghanistan: 1979 to Present.* New York: Columbia University Press.

—— (2007). "Kabul at War (1992–1996): State, Ethnicity and Social Classes." *South Asia Multidisciplinary Academic Journal.*

Dupree, L. (1959). "The Burqa Comes Off." American University's Field Staff Reports Service 3(2).

—— (1980). *Afghanistan*. Princeton, NJ: Princeton University Press.

Dupree, N. H. (1989). "Seclusion or Service: Will Women Have a Role in the Future of Afghanistan?" Occasional Paper # 29. New York: Afghanistan Forum.

—— (2008). *Afghanistan Over a Cup of Tea—46 Chronicles*. Stockholm: Swedish Committee for Afghanistan.

Dupree, N. H., et al. (1999). *Afghanistan Aid and the Taliban: Challenges on the Eve of the 21st Century*. Stockholm: Swedish Committee for Afghanistan.

Everson, R. (1997). Memo Regarding Mukrat Letter Reference Number 69 Dated July 16, 1997. Kabul: Agency Coordinating Body for Afghan Relief.

Fielden, M. (2001). Inter-agency Task Force Study on Taliban Decree and Its Implications. Pakistan: Inter-Agency Task Force.

Gutman, R. (2008). *How We Missed the Story*. Washington, DC: United States Institute of Peace.

Haqbeen, F.-R. (2000). From Agency Coordinating Body for Afghan Relief: Memo on Decree on Female Employment from Supreme Leader via MOP. A. Members.

Heisler, M., et al. (1999). "Health and Human Rights of Adolescent Girls in Afghanistan." *Journal of the American Medical Women's Association* 280: 462–64.

Hossain, M. K. (1999). *Interim Report on the Situation of Human Rights in Afghanistan*. Prepared by the Special Rapporteur of the Commission on Human Rights. New York: United Nations General Assembly.

—— (2000). *Interim Report of the Special Rapporteur of the Commission on Human Rights on the Situation of Human Rights in Afghanistan*. New York: United Nations General Assembly.

—— (2001). *Report on the Situation of Human Rights in Afghanistan*. Submitted by Mr. Kamal Hossain, Special Rapporteur, in Accordance with Commission Resolution 2000/18, United Nations. New York: United Nations General Assembly.

Howarth, A. (1993). *Hints for Working with Afghan Women in Purdah*. Kabul: Office of the UN High Commissioner for Refugees.

Human Rights Watch (2001). *Afghanistan: Humanity Denied— Systematic Violation of Women's Rights in Afghanistan*.

Johnson, C., and J. Leslie (2008). *Afghanistan: The Mirage of Peace*. New York: Zed.

Johnston, T. (1996). "Afghans Dig for Survival Through Kabul's Rubbish." *News-India Times*. December 27, 1996.

—— (1997). "Afghans Ban Women's Shoes." *Daily Telegraph* (Sydney). July 22, 1997.

—— (1997). "Food Shortage Discussed in Kabul." *News-India Times*. May 16, 1997.

—— (1997). "Women Losers in Iron Rule of Taleban." *Hobart Mercury*. April 4, 1997.

King, A. E. V. (1997). *Report of the United Nations Interagency Gender Mission to Afghanistan.* New York: United Nations.

Knabe, E. (1977). "Women in the Social Stratification of Afghanistan." In C.A.O. Van Nieuwenhuijze (ed.), *Commoners, Climbers, and Notables: A Sampler of Studies on Social Ranking in the Middle East*, pp. 329–59. Leiden: Brill.

Lancelot, A. (2008). *Burqas, foulards et minijupes: Paroles d'Afghanes.* Paris: Calmann-Levy.

Latifa (2001). *My Forbidden Face: Growing Up Under the Taliban: A Young Woman's Story.* New York: Hyperion.

Lowthian Bell, G. (1897). *Poems from the Divan of Hafiz.* London: William Heinemann. Reprinted by BiblioLife, LLC.

Mail listing newsletter for F. A. Gulalai Habib (1997). Kabul.

Maley, W. (1996). "Women and Public Policy in Afghanistan: A Comment." *World Development* 24(1): 203–6.

—— ed. (1998). *Fundamentalism Reborn? Afghanistan and the Taliban.* New York: New York University Press.

Mamnoon, F. (2000). Memo on Resolution of the Minister's Council of the Islamic Emirate of Afghanistan. A. Members. Peshawar and Kabul: Agency Coordinating Body for Afghan Relief.

Marsden, P. (1998). *The Taliban: War, Religion and the New Order in Afghanistan.* New York: Oxford University Press.

Matinuddin, K. (1999). *The Taliban Phenomenon: Afghanistan 1994–1997.* Oxford: Oxford University Press.

Matney, S. (2002). *Businesswomen in Kabul: A Study of the Economic Conditions for Female Entrepreneurs*. Kabul: Mercy Corps.

McCarthy, R. (2000). "Taliban Try to Scuttle 'Titanic' Craze." *Guardian* (London). December 10, 2000.

Medair (1997). Study of Health Provision and Needs in Kabul, Afghanistan. Kabul: Medair Afghanistan.

Mehta, S., ed. (2002). *Women for Afghan Women: Shattering Myths and Claiming the Future*. New York: Palgrave Macmillan.

Michel, A. A. (1959). *The Kabul, Kunduz and Helmand Valleys and the National Economy of Afghanistan*. Fifth in a Series of Reports. Washington, DC: National Academy of Sciences, National Research Council.

Mittra, Sangh, ed. (2004). *Encyclopedia of Women in South Asia: Afghanistan*. Delhi: Kalpaz.

Newberg, P. R. (1999). *Politics at the Heart: The Architecture of Humanitarian Assistance to Afghanistan. Paper No. 2*. Washington, DC: Carnegie Endowment for International Peace.

Niland, N. (2006). "Taliban-Run Afghanistan: The Politics of Closed Borders and Protection." In A. Bayefsky, ed., *Human Rights and Refugees, Internally Displaced Persons and Migrant Workers*, pp. 179–209. Koninklijke: Brill.

Nojumi, N. (2002). *The Rise of the Taliban in Afghanistan: Mass Mobilization, Civil War and the Future of the Region*. New York: Palgrave.

Organisation for Economic Co-operation and Development

(1999). *The Limits and Scope for the Use of Development Assistance Incentives and Disincentives for Influencing Conflict Situations—Case Study: Afghanistan*. Paris: Organisation for Economic Co-operation and Development.

Paik, C. H. (1997). *Final Report on the Situation of Human Rights in Afghanistan*. New York: United Nations.

Pont, A. M. (2001). *Blind Chickens and Social Animals: Creating Spaces for Afghan Women's Narratives Under the Taliban*. Portland, OR: Mercy Corps.

Qazizada, M. A. T. (2000). Further Memo on Female Employment. A. Members. Kabul, Islamic Emirate of Afghanistan Ministry of Planning.

Rashid, A. (2001). *Taliban: Militant Islam, Oil, and Fundamentalism in Central Asia*. New Haven, CT: Yale University Press.

—— (2008). *Descent into Chaos: The United States and the Failure of Nation Building in Pakistan, Afghanistan, and Central Asia*. London: Viking.

Reynolds, S. (1999). *Rebuilding Communities in the Urban Areas of Afghanistan: Symposium and Round Table on Operational Activities*. K. Riazi, United Nations Center for Human Settlements (UNCHS Habitat).

—— (2000). *Quarterly Report: Rebuilding Communities in Urban Afghanistan, July–September 2000*. United Nations Center for Human Settlements (UNCHS Habitat).

Rodey, B. J. (2000). *A Socio-economic Evaluation of the Community Forum Programme*, United Nations Centre for Human Settlements (UNCHS Habitat).

Rubin, B. R. (1997). "Women and Pipelines: Afghanistan's Proxy Wars." *International Affairs* (Royal Institute of International Affairs 1944– ) 73(2): 283–96.

—— (2002). *The Fragmentation of Afghanistan.* New Haven, CT: Yale University Press.

Samar, S., et al. (2002). *Afghanistan's Reform Agenda: Four Perspectives.* New York: Asia Society.

Seekins, D. M., and R. F. Nyrop (1986). *Afghanistan: A Country Study.* Washington, DC: The Studies.

Shahrani, M. N., and R. L. Canfield, eds. (1984). *Revolutions & Rebellions in Afghanistan.* Berkeley: University of California Institute of International Studies.

Shorish-Shamley, Ziebar (1998). *Report from Women's Alliance for Peace and Human Rights in Afghanistan.* Washington, DC.

Skaine, R. (2002). *The Women of Afghanistan Under the Taliban.* Jefferson, NC: McFarland.

Tavana, N., P. Cronin, and J. Alterman (1998). *The Taliban and Afghanistan: Implications for Regional Security and Options for International Action.* Special Report No. 39. Washington, DC: United States Institute of Peace.

United Nations Commission on Human Rights (1995). *Final Report on the Situation of Human Rights in Afghanistan.* Submitted by the Special Rapporteur, Mr. Felix Ermacora, in Accordance with Commission on Human Rights Resolution 1994/84. New York: United Nations Commission on Human Rights.

—— (1996). *Final Report on the Situation of Human Rights in Afghanistan*. Submitted by Mr. Choong-Hyun Paik, Special Rapporteur, in Accordance with Commission on Human Rights Resolution 1995/74. New York: United Nations Commission on Human Rights.

—— (1996). *Afghanistan: The Forgotten Crisis*. New York: United Nations Commission on Human Rights.

—— (1998). *Situation of Human Rights in Afghanistan: Report of the Secretary-General*. New York: United Nations Commission on Human Rights.

—— (2001). *Report of the Secretary-General on the Situation of Women and Girls in the Territories Occupied by Afghan Armed Groups*. Submitted in Accordance with Sub-commission Resolution 2000/11. New York: United Nations Commission on Human Rights.

Zhwak, M. Saeed (1995). *Women in Afghanistan History*. Peshawar: Katib Publishing Services.

Zoya, with J. Follain and R. Cristofari (2002). *Zoya's Story: An Afghan Woman's Struggle for Freedom*. New York: William Morrow.

# Resources

Below are just a few organizations about which you might be interested to learn more:

## Local organizations:

Afghanistan Center Kabul University
http://www.dupreefoundation.org/

Afghan Institute of Learning
http://www.afghaninstituteoflearning.org/

Afghan Women's Education Center
http://www.awec.info/

Afghan Women's Network
http://www.afghanwomensnetwork.org/

Afghan Women Skills Development Center
http://www.awsdc.net/

HAWCA
http://www.hawca.org/main/index.php

PARSA
http://www.afghanistan-parsa.org/

Voice of Women Organization
http://www.vwo.org.af/

Women for Afghan Women
http://www.womenforafghanwomen.org/

# *International organizations:*

Bpeace
http://www.bpeace.org

CARE
http://www.care.org/

Institute for Economic Empowerment of Women
(Peace Through Business)
http://www.ieew.org/

Mercy Corps
http://www.mercycorps.org/

Vital Voices
http://www.vitalvoices.org

Women for Women International
http://www.womenforwomen.org/

P.S.

Insights,
Interviews
& More...

## About the author

**2** Meet Gayle Tzemach Lemmon

**4** A Conversation with Gayle Lemmon

## About the book

**7** Lessons from *The Dressmaker*

## Read on

**9** A Reader's Guide: Questions and Topics for Discussion

**12** A Timeline of Afghan History: Events That Shaped Kamila's World

# Meet Gayle Tzemach Lemmon

GAYLE TZEMACH LEMMON is a contributing editor-at-large for *Newsweek* and *The Daily Beast*, reporting on economic and development issues with a focus on women, and the deputy director of the Council on Foreign Relations' Women and Foreign Policy Program. In 2004, after working for nearly a decade as a journalist with the ABC News Political Unit and *This Week with George Stephanopoulos*, she left ABC News to earn her MBA at Harvard, where she began writing about women entrepreneurs in conflict and post-conflict zones, including Afghanistan, Bosnia, and Rwanda.

© Jack Guy

Her reporting on entrepreneurs in these countries has been published by the *New York Times Global Edition*, *Financial Times*, *International Herald Tribune*, *Christian Science Monitor*, CNN.com, and *Daily Beast* as well as the World Bank and Harvard Business School. She has served as a Fulbright Scholar in Spain and a Robert Bosch Fellow in Germany. She speaks German, Spanish, French, and intermediate Dari, and lives in Los Angeles, California, where she spent the last several years working at the investment management firm PIMCO while writing *The Dressmaker of Khair Khana*. Gayle earned a BA in journalism summa cum laude from the University of Missouri School of Journalism and an MBA from Harvard Business School, where she received the 2006 Dean's Award for her work on women's entrepreneurship. She is a member of the International Center for Research on Women's New Leaders Circle and the Vital Voices Los Angeles Leadership Council. ∾

# A Conversation with Gayle Lemmon

*How have people responded to Kamila's story? Were you surprised by their response?*

I have been surprised and moved by how personally readers have taken Kamila's story. I have received notes from entrepreneurs who say that *The Dressmaker* has given them new inspiration to tackle their own challenges, and I have heard from fathers in Alaska who say that they want their daughters to share the values Kamila shows and shares in this story: love of family, desire to serve, and commitment to hard work. I also have heard from servicemen and women who say that this book gave them a look at Afghanistan they had never seen before. This is a war story, but it is also a family story and a business story, and I have been touched to see how much all of these have resonated with readers.

*Was writing the book an emotional journey?*

In many ways I grew up with this book. So many times I faced setbacks, whether it was due to the publishing schedule in New York or security challenges in Afghanistan, and I had to keep reminding myself just how much I believed in this universal story about what we do for those we love. I learned a great deal from those

66 This is a war story, but it is also a family story and a business story. 99

4

I spent time with in Afghanistan; they taught me about the power of family and the importance of grace under duress. Even when security was very bad in Kabul, and bombs and kidnappings were not unusual, they stayed focused on doing the best they could for those they loved and reminded me they had seen worse. The time I have spent in Afghanistan has made me more committed than ever to telling stories about the power and the resilience of the human spirit. There are so many unsung heroines and inspiring entrepreneurs all around us. And their stories are worth telling and sharing.

*Kamila's story is about sacrifice for one's family. You became a mother shortly after the publication of* The Dressmaker. *Does that change your understanding of the risks she took?*

I understood the risks before, but certainly having a child makes you even more intimately understand the power of family and the risks you are willing to take for those you love. Family is so central to the people in this story, who became an extended family for me, and I recognize more intimately than ever just what it means to do all you can to care for those who count on you.

*Were you surprised to see people in the business community embrace the book?*

I hoped that the business community would see that this is a story of the ▶

**66 There are so many unsung heroines and inspiring entrepreneurs all around us. 99**

power of entrepreneurs to change lives and create hope, so the fact that business leaders have embraced it has meant a great deal. Change will only come if people who have never thought about women and entrepreneurship see that women really are resources and have talents to be valued and invested in. Kamila's story is a testament to the power of entrepreneurs—women and men—to use business as a way to change lives for the better.

### What is Kamila doing now?

She is an entrepreneur working hard to create jobs and spread the word that business in Afghanistan has a bright future. She is among the most optimistic and determined business people I have ever met anywhere in the world. She believes strongly that Afghans can shape their own future using business to create a healthy economy that offers opportunity and a chance at a better and more peaceful tomorrow.

> Kamila's story is a testament to the power of entrepreneurs—women and men—to use business as a way to change lives for the better.

# Lessons from *The Dressmaker*

RESEARCHING AND WRITING *The Dressmaker of Khair Khana* taught me more than I will ever be able to eloquently express about grace, gratitude, and the universal power of the human spirit to triumph against dispiriting odds and daunting obstacles.

When I set out to write *The Dressmaker*, many people, including journalists, literary agents, and publishers, told me the public would have no interest in this story. People are tired of the war, they told me, and Afghanistan is too far away for people to recognize themselves in this story.

I never believed them because I felt certain that a story of family, faith, and perseverance would find a readership. I believed that women in particular were tired of reading "victim stories." Women everywhere in the world are used to taking hits and then getting back up because the people they love need and count on them. They are accustomed to receiving little credit and even less glory for the work they do every day to pull their families through impossible times. As I have seen in the several months since *The Dressmaker* met readers, they are ready to be acknowledged and to read a small story about a business that made a big difference at a desperate time.

Security was the biggest obstacle. I worried a great deal that my work put the young women I met at risk. But their courage was my inspiration. And so ▶

> 66 Many people, including journalists, literary agents, and publishers, told me the public would have no interest in this story. 99

when family and friends told me I was mad to get married one month before I left, yet again, for Afghanistan, I ignored them. When setbacks came and I felt despondent and beaten, certain that this book would never reach readers, I reminded myself that the young women I had the privilege of getting to know had taken on far greater challenges and faced risks far larger than any I knew.

All of us who spend time in parts of the world where war has had its way are changed by it. We feel humbled by the resilience of those around us, guilty for going home to safer spots, and more committed to telling stories that might otherwise never reach our audiences. I certainly feel all of these. And I am humbled by the generosity of people who had very little by a rich country's standards of wealth, but who gave me their time, their hospitality, and their stories.

Meeting readers moved by this story has moved me because it has reminded me once again that the personal is very deeply universal. Nearly everyone has a mother or an aunt or a grandmother or a sister who has sacrificed for them and taken risks. The backdrop and degree of danger they faced may be different than it was for Kamila, but the principle is the same. All around us are unsung heroines and inspiring entrepreneurs who merit our attention, our investment, and our celebration. Bringing *The Dressmaker* to life was part of honoring those heroines in my own life and of sharing a story that proves the power to change our world that each of us, no matter who or where we are, possesses. ◠

# A Reader's Guide
## Questions and Topics for Discussion

1. Kamila studied to become a teacher and even earned a prestigious teaching certificate. Before she could complete her training, the Taliban took over Kabul and banned women from nearly all public places, including schools. How did Kamila adapt the skills she learned as a teacher and put them to use starting her dressmaking business, and later in her UN work?

2. At many crucial junctures, Kamila turns to her faith for guidance. What role does faith play in her personal journey?

3. Under the Taliban, Afghan women were confined to their homes and saw their lives transformed virtually overnight. Yet many women like Kamila still needed to support their families, and so they found creative ways to work within and around these new restrictions. What would you have done under similar circumstances? Would you have dared to go against the Taliban's rules at the risk of your own safety?

4. Malika plays an instrumental role in teaching Kamila how to sew and in getting her dressmaking business off the ground. Kamila often seeks out the advice of her eldest sister, even though she doesn't always take it. ▶

How would you characterize the relationship between these two sisters? What role do you think this relationship played in Kamila's business success?

5. Lemmon paints a colorful yet nuanced portrait of modern-day Afghanistan. The story of Kamila and her family presents an alternative to the conventional image of women as victims of war. Did Lemmon's portrayal change the way you think about Afghanistan? Or about women and war?

6. Within a year, Kamila was able to transform a living room operation into a thriving dressmaking business, selling finely embroidered dresses to tailors throughout Kabul and providing meaningful work for an entire community of women. What do you think about Kamila's business practices? Why do you think she and her sisters were so successful? What lessons about entrepreneurship can be taken from their story?

7. In chapter 7, Kamila and her sisters work around the clock to make six dresses for a wedding party, only to discover that the bride is marrying a Talib. How does this episode impact you or cause you to revisit your view of the Taliban? If Taliban soldiers knew about the Sidiqi sisters' tailoring business, why didn't they shut it down? What did you think when you saw that there were

Taliban who sent their daughters to work with Kamila?

8. How does Lemmon portray men throughout the book? Think of Rahim, Mr. Sidiqi, Ali and his brothers, and the Talibs Kamila encounters. Do these characters reshape or reinforce your impressions of men in Afghanistan?

9. Despite being faced with the daily perils of war and economic hardships, the Sidiqi family never completely abandons their home in Khair Khana. What does that say about their commitment to their community? To their country?

10. How does Kamila's story affect the way you see the future of Afghanistan and America's presence in this war-scarred country? ∽

# A Timeline of Afghan History
## Events That Shaped Kamila's World

**1973:** Mohammad Zahir Shah is overthrown in a military coup. Mohammad Daoud Khan becomes president.

**1978:** Daoud Khan is deposed in a communist coup. Nur Mohammad Taraki becomes president, and Babrak Karmal is named deputy prime minister. Taraki signs a friendship treaty with the Soviet Union.

**1979:** President Nur Mohammad Taraki is killed, and Hafizullah Amin becomes president. Soviet forces invade Kabul and execute Amin. Former Deputy Prime Minister Babrak Karmal becomes president. The Soviet invasion and installation of Karmal ignites violent public protests. Soviet War in Afghanistan begins.

**1980:** Mujahideen fight against the Soviet military and the USSR-backed Afghan army.

**1986:** Prime Minister Babrak Karmal is replaced by Muhammad Najibullah, former chief of the Afghan secret police.

**1988:** The U.S., Pakistan, Afghanistan, and the Soviet Union sign the Geneva Accords, ending the Soviet occupation and war in Afghanistan.

**1989–92:** Following Soviet withdrawal, the Mujahideen continue their resistance against Soviet-supported President Muhammad Najibullah.

**1992:** The Northern Alliance is formed. The Mujahideen overthrow President Muhammad Najibullah and Burhanuddin Rabbani becomes president. The Afghan Civil War begins.

**1994:** Taliban seize Kandahar, Lashkargah, and Helmand.

**1995:** Taliban capture Herat. Conservative, traditional dress for both men and women is enforced. Women are required to be completed covered; they cannot travel outside the home without a male chaperone (*mahram*). Women are banned from working, and girls' schools are closed.

**1996:** Taliban take Kabul. Former President Muhammad Najibullah is publicly executed.

**2000:** UN Resolution 1333 imposes an arms ban on the Taliban. UN Resolution 1325 is unanimously adopted calling for women's full and equal participation in peace processes and the protection of women in armed conflicts.

**March 2001:** Despite international protests, the Taliban destroy historical Buddhist relics in Bamiyan, Afghanistan.

**September 9, 2001:** Ahmad Shah Massoud, head of the Northern Alliance, is assassinated.

**September 11, 2001:** Al-Qaeda hijackers crash commercial airplanes into the World Trade Center, the Pentagon, and a Pennsylvania field, killing thousands. Osama bin Laden and ▶

al-Qaeda claim responsibility for the attacks.

**October 7, 2001:** The Taliban refuse to hand over bin Laden; U.S. forces invade Afghanistan.

**November 13, 2001:** The Northern Alliance enters Kabul, and the Taliban flee south.

**December 2001:** The Bonn conference establishes a political blueprint for Afghanistan, leading to elections in 2004. Taliban leaders surrender their final Afghan territory, the province of Zabul. ∾